Bull,

Bear,

and

Beyond

of Indian Share Market

Welcome to the dynamic world of the

Indian share market – a realm where Bulls and Bears dance to the rhythm of economic trends, investor sentiments, and global influences. In this comprehensive ebook, "Bulls, Bears, and Beyond of Indian Share Market," we embark on a journey that transcends the ordinary, delving into the intricacies of one of the most vibrant financial landscapes in the world.

Unlock the secrets of financial success with "Mastering the Market." This comprehensive guide takes you on a journey through the dynamic landscape of the Indian share market, providing you with the tools to navigate the highs and lows of Bulls, Bears, and Beyond. Whether you're a seasoned investor or a novice, this ebook is your key to understanding and thriving in the ever-evolving world of finance.

■ Why You Need This Book:

- Gain insights into market trends and strategies that work in the Indian context.
- Learn how to leverage the power of Bulls and navigate the challenges posed by Bears.
- Explore advanced techniques that go beyond the basics, ensuring you stay ahead of the market curve.

🔦 What's Inside:

- 34 comprehensive chapters covering everything from market fundamentals to advanced trading/Investing strategies.
- In-depth analysis of the top 30 questions most people ask about the Indian share market.
- Actionable insights from industry experts to guide you through every aspect of your investment journey.

Book Introduction:

Welcome to the exciting world of Indian share market investing! In "Mastering the Market," we embark on a journey that transcends the conventional boundaries of Bulls and Bears. This ebook is not just a guide; it's your passport to financial empowerment.

With over 100 pages of meticulously researched content, we delve into the nuances of the Indian share market, offering you a roadmap to navigate the complexities and capitalize on opportunities. Each chapter is crafted to provide you with actionable insights, ensuring that you not only understand the market but thrive in it.

Are you ready to master the market? Let's dive into the Bulls, Bears, and Beyond of the Indian share market together!

Chapter 1: Introduction to Indian Share Market

Welcome to the heart of financial opportunities – the Indian share market. In this chapter, we embark on a journey that demystifies the intricate workings of the market, providing you with a solid foundation for your investment endeavors.

Understanding the Market Landscape

To navigate the Indian share market, one must first understand its landscape. We'll explore the key players, including stock exchanges, regulatory bodies, and market participants. By unraveling the interconnected web of entities shaping the market, you'll gain a comprehensive overview of its structure.

Historical Evolution

Dive into the rich history of the Indian share market, tracing its evolution from the early days to the modern, technology-driven era. Understanding the historical context is crucial for interpreting market trends and making informed predictions about its future.

Market Segments

The Indian share market comprises various segments, each with its unique characteristics. From equities and commodities to derivatives, we'll delve into the diverse array of investment options available, ensuring you can tailor your portfolio to your financial goals.

Investment Objectives and Risk Appetite

Before venturing into the market, it's essential to define your investment objectives and assess your risk tolerance. We'll guide you through this self-discovery process, helping you align your investment strategy with your financial aspirations.

Market Participants and Their Roles

Who are the major players influencing the market, and what roles do they play? From retail investors to institutional giants, understanding the dynamics between different market participants is crucial for predicting market movements.

The Role of Technology

In today's digital age, technology plays a pivotal role in shaping the market landscape. We'll explore how advancements in technology, algorithmic trading, and online platforms have revolutionized the way investors engage with the market.

Regulatory Framework

Navigate the regulatory landscape governing the Indian share market. Learn about the roles of regulatory bodies like SEBI (Securities and Exchange Board of India) and how they ensure fair and transparent market practices.

Market Indices and Benchmarks

Explore the significance of market indices as benchmarks for evaluating overall market performance. Understanding indices like the Nifty and Sensex will empower you to gauge market trends and make informed investment decisions.

Setting the Stage for Your Journey

As we conclude this chapter, you'll have gained a solid understanding of the Indian share market's foundations. Armed with this knowledge, you're ready to venture into the subsequent chapters, where we delve deeper into the intricacies of Bulls, Bears, and the dynamic landscape beyond. Get ready to embark on a transformative journey into the heart of financial markets!

Chapter 2: Understanding Bulls and Bears

Unveiling Market Forces

Welcome to the fundamental dichotomy that defines market movements – Bulls and Bears. Understanding their nature is the first step in navigating the dynamic landscape of the Indian share market.

Bulls: Charging Ahead with Optimism

Bulls symbolize optimism and confidence in the market. In a bull market, prices are on the rise, and investors expect further gains. Bullish investors believe in the economic outlook, leading to increased buying activity. The upward momentum is characterized by sustained optimism, positive economic indicators, and a generally favorable investment climate.

Bears: Dominating in Pessimism

Contrary to Bulls, Bears represent pessimism and a lack of confidence in the market. A bear market is characterized by falling prices, and investors anticipate further declines. Bearish sentiments prevail due to economic concerns, geopolitical tensions, or other factors leading to a negative outlook. During a bear market, selling pressure intensifies, resulting in a downward spiral.

Market Trends and Strategies

Navigating the interplay between Bulls and Bears is crucial for investors. Bull markets offer opportunities for capitalizing on upward trends, while bear markets require strategies to protect investments and identify potential buying opportunities.

Riding the Waves: Strategies for Bulls and Bears

Bullish Strategies
- Buy and Hold: Capitalize on the upward trend by holding onto quality stocks for the long term.
- Growth Investing: Identify companies with strong growth potential and promising future earnings.

Bearish Strategies
- Short Selling: Profit from falling prices by selling borrowed shares and buying them back at a lower price.
- Defensive Stocks: Invest in sectors resistant to economic downturns, such as utilities and healthcare.

Mastering Bull and Bear Markets

Successful investors recognize that both Bull and Bear markets are inherent to the market cycle. The key lies in adapting strategies to market conditions, staying informed, and maintaining a disciplined approach to achieve financial goals.

In the upcoming chapters, we'll delve deeper into market dynamics, providing insights into economic indicators, global influences, and strategies to navigate the volatility presented by Bulls and Bears. Get ready to elevate your understanding of the Indian share market!

Chapter 3: Decoding Bulls and Bears

Welcome to the rollercoaster ride of market emotions, where Bulls charge ahead with optimism, and Bears bring a sense of caution. In this chapter, we delve into the dichotomy of Bulls and Bears, understanding their impact on market trends and, ultimately, your investment portfolio.

The Dance of Bulls: Riding the Upswing

Bulls symbolize a market on the rise, characterized by optimism, increasing stock prices, and a general sense of confidence. We explore the factors driving Bull markets, such as economic growth, positive corporate earnings, and favorable market sentiment. Learn how to identify the signs of a Bull market and position your investments for maximum returns.

The Roar of Bears: Navigating the Downturn

Bears, on the other hand, signal a market in decline. Understanding the key indicators of a Bear market – economic downturns, falling corporate profits, and negative investor sentiment – is crucial for protecting your portfolio. We guide you through strategies to weather the storm when Bears dominate the market landscape.

Bull vs. Bear: Analyzing Market Trends

Dive into the technical and fundamental indicators that help distinguish between Bull and Bear markets. From chart patterns and moving averages to economic indicators and earnings reports, we equip you with the tools to interpret market trends accurately.

Bullish and Bearish Strategies

Explore specific investment strategies tailored for Bull and Bear markets. Discover how to capitalize on upward momentum during Bull markets and safeguard your investments during Bear markets. A well-rounded understanding of these strategies will empower you to adapt to ever-changing market conditions.

Bull-Bear Transitions: Navigating Market Cycles

Markets are dynamic, and transitions between Bulls and Bears are inevitable. Gain insights into market cycles, understanding the phases of expansion, peak, contraction, and trough. Recognizing these cycles will enable you to anticipate market shifts and adjust your investment strategy accordingly.

Sentiment Analysis: The Pulse of the Market

Uncover the power of sentiment analysis in gauging market mood. Learn how social media, news sentiment, and investor surveys can provide valuable insights into the prevailing sentiment, helping you stay ahead of market movements.

Bull and Bear Market Case Studies

Delve into real-world case studies of iconic Bull and Bear markets. By analyzing historical market events, you'll gain a deeper understanding of the factors influencing market trends and the strategies employed by successful investors during these periods.

Developing Your Bull-Bear Strategy

As we conclude this chapter, you'll be equipped with a nuanced understanding of Bulls and Bears. More importantly, you'll have the knowledge to develop a robust strategy that aligns with the prevailing market conditions. The journey through the Indian share market continues, and you're well-prepared to navigate the twists and turns that lie ahead. Stay tuned for the chapters that delve deeper into market fundamentals and advanced trading strategies!

Chapter 4: Market Fundamentals

Welcome to the cornerstone of successful investing –

understanding the fundamentals of the Indian share market. In this chapter, we'll delve into the core principles that drive market dynamics, providing you with the essential knowledge to make informed investment decisions.

Anatomy of Stock Trading

Grasp the basics of stock trading, from the mechanics of buying and selling to the role of brokers and trading platforms. We break down the jargon, ensuring you have a solid foundation for navigating the complexities of the stock market.

Types of Investments

Explore the diverse array of investment options available in the Indian share market. From stocks and bonds to mutual funds and exchange-traded funds (ETFs), we guide you through the characteristics and potential returns of each, helping you build a diversified investment portfolio.

Risk and Reward: The Investor's Dilemma

Understand the fundamental principle of risk and reward in investing. We'll explore the concept of risk tolerance and how it influences your investment decisions. Learn to strike the right balance between risk and reward to achieve your financial goals.

Market Order vs. Limit Order

Navigate the nuances of market orders and limit orders. Discover when to use each type of order to optimize your trade execution and minimize slippage, ensuring you get the best possible prices for your investments.

Understanding Market Indices

Dive into the world of market indices, such as the Nifty and Sensex, and understand their significance as benchmarks for evaluating market performance. Learn how these indices reflect the overall health of the market and guide investment strategies.

Dividends and Corporate Actions

Explore the impact of dividends and corporate actions on your investments. Understand how dividend payouts, stock splits, and bonus issues can influence stock prices and your overall portfolio returns.

Initial Public Offerings (IPOs)

Uncover the opportunities presented by IPOs in the primary market. Learn how companies go public, the process of IPOs, and how investors can participate in these offerings to capitalize on early-stage growth.

Secondary Market Offerings

Navigate the dynamics of secondary market offerings, including rights issues and follow-on public offerings (FPOs). Understand how these offerings can affect stock prices and provide opportunities for investors to enhance their portfolios.

Sectoral Analysis

Delve into the importance of sectoral analysis in identifying investment opportunities. Understand how economic and industry trends impact specific sectors, allowing you to make informed decisions based on the broader market context.

Long-Term vs. Short-Term Investing

Evaluate the pros and cons of long-term and short-term investing strategies. Discover how your investment horizon influences your approach to risk, portfolio composition, and overall investment philosophy.

Setting Your Investment Goals

As we conclude this chapter, take the time to define your investment goals. Whether it's wealth accumulation, retirement planning, or funding a specific life goal, understanding your objectives is the first step towards crafting a personalized and effective investment strategy. The journey through the Indian share market continues, and armed with fundamental knowledge, you're ready to explore advanced strategies in the chapters that follow. Stay tuned for insights into navigating Bull and Bear markets, advanced trading techniques, and more!

Chapter 5: Decoding Market Dynamics

The Dance of Economic Indicators

Welcome to the intricate dance of market dynamics, where economic indicators, global events, and investor sentiments converge to shape the movements of the Indian share market.

Economic Indicators: Unveiling Market Trends

GDP Growth Rates
- Explore the impact of Gross Domestic Product (GDP) growth rates on market trends. A growing economy often translates to bullish sentiments, while economic contractions may signal a bearish phase.

Inflation Rates
- Delve into the relationship between inflation rates and the stock market. Moderate inflation may be conducive to a bullish market, while high inflation can introduce uncertainties and impact investor confidence.

Interest Rates
- Understand the influence of interest rates on market dynamics. Lower interest rates typically favor bullish trends by encouraging borrowing and spending, while higher rates may have a bearish effect.

Global Events: A Ripple Effect

Geopolitical Events
- Explore how geopolitical events can send ripples through the market. Political stability or instability, trade agreements, and diplomatic relations can significantly impact investor sentiments.

Global Economic Trends

- Understand the interconnectedness of the global economy. Changes in major economies, trade balances, and international monetary policies can influence the Indian share market.

Investor Sentiments: The Human Element

Market Sentiment Indicators
- Delve into market sentiment indicators, such as the Volatility Index (VIX) and surveys gauging investor optimism or pessimism. These indicators offer insights into the collective mood of the market.

Behavioral Finance Factors
- Explore the role of behavioral finance in market dynamics. Investor behavior, influenced by emotions and cognitive biases, can contribute to market trends and fluctuations.

Navigating Market Dynamics with Strategy

Tactical Asset Allocation
- Understand the concept of tactical asset allocation. This strategy involves adjusting portfolio weights based on short-term market conditions, allowing investors to respond to changing dynamics.

Contrarian Investing
- Explore contrarian investing, a strategy that involves going against prevailing market sentiments. Contrarians believe that markets overreact to news, presenting opportunities for strategic investments.

The Holistic Approach to Market Dynamics

Successful navigation of market dynamics requires a holistic understanding. Investors who grasp the interplay between economic indicators, global events, and investor sentiments can position themselves strategically to ride the waves of the Indian share market.

In the following chapters, we'll delve deeper into strategies for managing volatility, incorporating fundamental and technical analysis, and mastering the psychology of market participants. Get ready to unravel the layers of market dynamics and enhance your prowess in the world of Indian share trading!

Chapter 6: Strategies for Bull Markets

Welcome to the exhilarating world of Bull markets, where optimism reigns, and opportunities abound. In this chapter, we'll unravel the strategies that savvy investors employ to capitalize on the upward momentum of Bull markets, ensuring you can navigate these bullish phases with confidence.

Riding the Bull: Key Characteristics

Understand the key characteristics of Bull markets, from rising stock prices and strong economic indicators to high investor confidence. We'll explore how to identify the early signs of a Bull market and position your portfolio for maximum growth.

Growth Stocks and Momentum Investing

Dive into the world of growth stocks and momentum investing. Learn how to identify companies with the potential for substantial earnings growth and capitalize on the momentum created by positive market sentiment.

Sector Rotation Strategies

Explore sector rotation as a dynamic strategy to capitalize on Bull markets. Discover how to identify sectors poised for growth and strategically rotate your investments to align with the prevailing market trends.

Leveraging Technical Analysis

Master the art of technical analysis as a tool for navigating Bull markets. From chart patterns and trend analysis to oscillators and indicators, we'll guide you through the techniques that help you make informed decisions during upward market trends.

IPO Opportunities in Bull Markets

Uncover the unique opportunities presented by initial public offerings (IPOs) during Bull markets. Understand how companies capitalize on positive market sentiment to go public and explore strategies for participating in these offerings.

Bullish Options Trading Strategies

Delve into options trading strategies tailored for Bull markets. From covered calls to bullish spreads, we'll explore how options can be used to enhance returns and manage risk in a rising market environment.

Dividend Growth Investing

Explore the benefits of dividend growth investing during Bull markets. Discover how dividend-paying stocks can provide a steady income stream while offering the potential for capital appreciation in positive market conditions.

Tactical Asset Allocation

Understand the importance of tactical asset allocation in optimizing your portfolio during Bull markets. Learn how to strategically allocate your assets across different classes to maximize returns while managing risk.

Behavioral Finance in Bull Markets

Explore the psychological aspects of investing during Bull markets. Understand how investor sentiment and behavioral biases can impact decision-making and learn strategies to stay disciplined in the face of market exuberance.

Setting Realistic Profit Targets

As you navigate Bull markets, it's essential to set realistic profit targets. We'll guide you through the process of establishing achievable goals and implementing disciplined strategies to lock in gains while the market is favorable.

Continuous Learning and Adaptation

Concluding this chapter, we emphasize the importance of continuous learning and adaptation. Bull markets evolve, and staying informed about market trends, economic indicators, and emerging opportunities is crucial for sustained success. Armed with these strategies, you're well-prepared to thrive in Bull markets. Stay tuned as we delve into the strategies for navigating Bear markets in the next chapter!

Chapter 7: Navigating Volatility with Confidence

Embracing the Market Rollercoaster

Welcome to the rollercoaster ride of market volatility – a phenomenon that tests the mettle of investors. In this chapter, we'll explore the nature of volatility, its causes, and strategies to navigate the unpredictable twists and turns with confidence.

Understanding Market Volatility

Defining Volatility
- Explore the concept of volatility, which measures the degree of variation in a trading price series over time. Volatility reflects market uncertainty and is a crucial aspect of the investment landscape.

Causes of Volatility
- Delve into the various factors that contribute to market volatility. From economic indicators and geopolitical events to sudden shifts in investor sentiments, understanding the root causes is key.

Strategies for Managing Volatility

Diversification
- Embrace the power of diversification to mitigate the impact of volatility. By spreading investments across different asset classes, industries, and geographical regions, investors can reduce overall portfolio risk.

Use of Stop-Loss Orders

- Implement stop-loss orders to protect against significant losses. These orders automatically trigger a sale when a stock reaches a predetermined price, helping investors limit potential downside.

Volatility Index (VIX) as a Guide
- Understand the Volatility Index (VIX) as a gauge of market expectations. Monitoring the VIX can provide insights into the anticipated level of market volatility, helping investors adjust their strategies accordingly.

Seizing Opportunities Amid Volatility

Value Investing During Dips
- Explore the concept of value investing during market downturns. Volatility can create opportunities to acquire fundamentally sound stocks at discounted prices.

Contrarian Strategies
- Adopt contrarian strategies during periods of extreme volatility. Contrarians may view market panics as opportunities to go against the prevailing sentiment, anticipating a potential rebound.

The Role of Risk Management

Setting Realistic Expectations
- Manage volatility by setting realistic expectations. Understanding that market fluctuations are inherent helps investors maintain a long-term perspective and avoid making impulsive decisions.

Regular Portfolio Reviews
- Conduct regular reviews of your portfolio to assess its resilience to volatility. Adjust your holdings based on changing market conditions and your risk tolerance.

The Path to Confident Investing

Navigating volatility requires a combination of strategic planning, risk management, and a disciplined approach. As we move forward, we'll delve into more advanced strategies, incorporating fundamental and technical analysis, to further enhance your confidence in the face of market uncertainties. Get ready to elevate your understanding and mastery of the Indian share market!

Chapter 8: Surviving Bear Markets

Welcome to the challenging yet opportunistic terrain of

Bear markets. In this chapter, we'll explore strategies designed to help you not only weather the storm but also identify opportunities amid the downturns. Surviving Bear markets requires resilience, strategic thinking, and a keen understanding of risk management.

Recognizing Bear Market Indicators

Understand the early warning signs of a Bear market, from declining stock prices and economic contractions to negative investor sentiment. We'll equip you with the tools to identify and interpret these indicators, enabling you to act proactively when faced with an impending Bear market.

Defensive Stock Strategies

Explore defensive stock strategies tailored for Bear markets. Discover sectors and industries that historically demonstrate resilience during economic downturns and learn how to position your portfolio to mitigate losses.

Value Investing in Bear Markets

Dive into the principles of value investing and how they can be applied strategically during Bear markets. Learn to identify undervalued stocks with strong fundamentals, offering potential for long-term gains when the market rebounds.

Short Selling and Hedging Techniques

Explore the world of short selling and hedging as strategies to profit from falling markets and protect your portfolio during Bear markets. We'll guide you through the mechanics and risks associated with these advanced techniques.

Cash Management and Liquidity

Understand the importance of cash management and liquidity during Bear markets. Learn how to maintain sufficient cash reserves to capitalize on investment opportunities that may arise amid market downturns.

Opportunistic Buying in Bear Markets

Discover the art of opportunistic buying during Bear markets. We'll explore how to identify bargains in a bearish market, strategically adding undervalued assets to your portfolio for potential future gains.

Asset Allocation Strategies for Bears

Delve into asset allocation strategies specifically designed for Bear markets. Learn how to reallocate your portfolio to minimize losses and position yourself for a potential market recovery.

Behavioral Finance in Bear Markets

Explore the psychological aspects of investing during Bear markets. Understand common behavioral biases that can lead to irrational decision-making and learn strategies to maintain discipline and avoid panic selling.

Leveraging Options for Downside Protection

Understand how options can be used as a tool for downside protection during Bear markets. From protective puts to bearish spreads, explore options strategies that can help safeguard your portfolio in adverse market conditions.

Risk Management in Bear Markets

Master the art of risk management during Bear markets. Learn how to assess and manage risk effectively, setting stop-loss orders and implementing other risk mitigation techniques to protect your capital.

Building Resilience: Lessons from Bear Market History

Explore historical Bear markets and the lessons they offer. Analyze how successful investors navigated these challenging periods and extract valuable insights that can inform your approach to Bear markets.

Staying Informed: Monitoring Economic Indicators

As we conclude this chapter, emphasize the importance of staying informed by monitoring key economic indicators. Understanding the broader economic landscape can provide valuable insights into the duration and severity of Bear markets, aiding in strategic decision-making. Armed with these survival strategies, you're well-prepared to navigate the uncertainties of Bear markets and position yourself for long-term success. Stay tuned for the next chapters where we explore advanced trading strategies, technical analysis, and the psychology of trading.

Chapter 9: Investor's Toolkit - Fundamental Analysis

Peeling Back the Layers of Fundamental Analysis

In this chapter, we venture into the fundamental analysis toolkit, an essential set of skills for investors seeking to understand the intrinsic value of a company. By dissecting financial statements, economic indicators, and industry trends, fundamental analysis provides a comprehensive view of potential investments.

The Foundations of Fundamental Analysis

Evaluating Financial Statements
- Delve into the analysis of income statements, balance sheets, and cash flow statements. Understand how these financial documents reveal a company's profitability, financial health, and ability to generate cash.

Assessing Earnings Per Share (EPS)
- Explore the significance of Earnings Per Share (EPS) as a key metric. EPS reflects a company's profitability on a per-share basis, helping investors gauge its earning potential.

Economic Indicators and Industry Trends

Impact of Economic Indicators
- Understand how economic indicators, such as interest rates, inflation, and GDP, influence fundamental analysis. Economic conditions can affect a company's performance and overall market dynamics.

Industry and Market Analysis
- Explore the importance of industry and market analysis. Identifying trends, competitive landscapes, and growth potential within specific sectors enhances the accuracy of fundamental assessments.

Valuation Techniques

Price-to-Earnings (P/E) Ratio
- Uncover the significance of the Price-to-Earnings (P/E) ratio. This metric compares a company's stock price to its earnings, providing insights into its valuation relative to industry peers.

Discounted Cash Flow (DCF) Analysis
- Dive into Discounted Cash Flow (DCF) analysis as a method to estimate the intrinsic value of a company. By forecasting future cash flows and discounting them to present value, investors can determine a fair valuation.

ESG Considerations

Environmental, Social, and Governance (ESG) Criteria
- Embrace the incorporation of ESG criteria into fundamental analysis. Evaluating a company's commitment to environmental sustainability, social responsibility, and strong governance can provide a more holistic view.

ESG Reporting and Impact on Investment Decisions
- Explore how companies' ESG reporting practices impact investment decisions. Investors increasingly consider ethical and sustainable practices when making long-term investment choices.

Case Studies in Fundamental Analysis

Real-World Applications
- Analyze real-world case studies to witness how fundamental analysis principles are applied. From evaluating financial statements to making investment decisions, these cases offer practical insights.

Interactive Exercises
- Engage in interactive exercises to sharpen your fundamental analysis skills. Practice analyzing financial statements, interpreting economic indicators, and valuing companies using the tools provided.

Mastery of Fundamental Analysis

As we conclude this chapter, remember that fundamental analysis is a powerful tool for investors seeking a deeper understanding of the companies they invest in. In the upcoming chapters, we'll delve into the world of technical analysis, combining both approaches to enhance your decision-making prowess in the Indian share market. Get ready to elevate your analytical skills!

Chapter 10: Fundamental Analysis - Digging Deeper

Welcome to the foundation of sound investing -

fundamental analysis. In this chapter, we'll embark on a journey to uncover the deeper layers of company valuation, financial health assessment, and the factors that drive stock prices in the Indian share market.

Analyzing Financial Statements

Dive into the core of fundamental analysis by dissecting financial statements. Explore balance sheets, income statements, and cash flow statements, deciphering the financial health of companies and gaining insights into their performance.

Key Financial Ratios

Master the art of using financial ratios to assess a company's profitability, liquidity, and overall efficiency. From price-to-earnings ratio (P/E) to return on equity (ROE), understand how these ratios provide valuable benchmarks for investment decisions.

Earnings Reports and Corporate Guidance

Explore the impact of earnings reports and corporate guidance on stock prices. Learn how to interpret financial results, analyze management guidance, and assess the implications for a company's future growth potential.

Dividend Analysis and Share Buybacks

Delve into the world of dividend analysis and share buybacks. Understand how a company's dividend history and buyback programs can provide insights into its financial stability and commitment to returning value to shareholders.

Economic Indicators and Industry Analysis

Expand your fundamental analysis toolkit by incorporating economic indicators and industry analysis. Learn how macroeconomic factors and industry trends influence company performance, helping you identify sectors with growth potential.

Qualitative Factors: Management and Governance

Explore qualitative factors that contribute to a company's success. Assess the quality of management, corporate governance practices, and the company's strategic vision to make informed decisions about long-term investments.

Understanding Debt and Leverage

Uncover the nuances of debt and leverage in fundamental analysis. Learn how to evaluate a company's debt levels, assess its ability to service debt, and understand the impact of leverage on overall financial health.

Cash Flow Analysis

Master the intricacies of cash flow analysis. Explore operating, investing, and financing cash flows, understanding how cash flow metrics provide insights into a company's ability to generate and manage cash effectively.

Valuation Models: DCF and Comparable Analysis

Dive into advanced valuation models, including discounted cash flow (DCF) analysis and comparable company analysis. Learn how to estimate a company's intrinsic value by forecasting future cash flows and comparing it to similar companies in the market.

Event-Driven Investing: Mergers, Acquisitions, and IPOs

Explore event-driven investing opportunities arising from mergers, acquisitions, and initial public offerings (IPOs). Understand how these corporate events can impact stock prices and present opportunities for strategic investment.

Environmental, Social, and Governance (ESG) Analysis

Delve into the emerging field of ESG analysis. Understand how environmental, social, and governance factors can influence a company's long-term performance and why incorporating ESG considerations is becoming increasingly important for investors.

International Financial Reporting Standards (IFRS)

Explore the impact of International Financial Reporting Standards (IFRS) on fundamental analysis. Understand the global accounting standards that companies adhere to and how these standards affect financial statement interpretation.

Risk Management in Fundamental Analysis

As we conclude this chapter, we'll focus on risk management within the realm of fundamental analysis. Learn how to identify and mitigate risks associated with investments, ensuring a well-balanced and informed approach to building and managing your investment portfolio. Stay tuned for the next chapters where we explore options and futures trading, risk management strategies, and the psychology of trading.

Chapter 11: Investor's Toolkit - Technical Analysis

Decoding Market Trends with Technical Analysis

Welcome to the fascinating realm of technical analysis, a toolkit that empowers investors to analyze historical price movements, identify patterns, and make informed predictions about future market trends. In this chapter, we'll explore the intricacies of technical analysis and how it complements fundamental analysis in the quest for successful investing.

The Foundations of Technical Analysis

Price Patterns and Trends
- Uncover the significance of price patterns and trends in technical analysis. From support and resistance levels to trendlines, understanding these elements is crucial for predicting market movements.

Chart Types and Their Applications
- Explore different chart types, such as line charts, bar charts, and candlestick charts. Learn how each type provides unique insights into price movements and market psychology.

Technical Indicators

Moving Averages

- Dive into moving averages as a key technical indicator. Explore how simple and exponential moving averages smooth out price data, revealing underlying trends and potential reversal points.

Relative Strength Index (RSI)
- Understand the Relative Strength Index (RSI) as a momentum indicator. RSI helps identify overbought or oversold conditions, offering insights into potential trend reversals.

Japanese Candlestick Patterns

Bullish and Bearish Candlestick Patterns
- Delve into the world of Japanese candlestick patterns. Recognize bullish patterns, such as engulfing and hammer, as well as bearish patterns, like shooting star and evening star, to anticipate price movements.

Candlestick Pattern Recognition
- Learn how to recognize and interpret candlestick patterns in real-time. Engage in exercises that enhance your ability to identify these patterns and make timely decisions.

Support and Resistance Strategies

Role of Support and Resistance
- Explore the critical roles of support and resistance levels in technical analysis. Discover how these levels act as barriers to price movements and can guide entry and exit points.

Trendline Analysis
- Master the art of trendline analysis. Understand how drawing trendlines on charts helps identify the direction of the market trend and potential trend reversals.

Integrating Fundamental and Technical Analysis

Holistic Investment Approach
- Embrace the synergy of fundamental and technical analysis. Learn how integrating both approaches can provide a comprehensive view, enhancing the precision of investment decisions.

Case Studies in Combined Analysis
- Explore case studies that showcase the power of combining fundamental and technical analysis. Witness how investors use both toolkits to navigate the complexities of the Indian share market.

Continuous Learning in Technical Analysis

Staying Updated on Chart Patterns

- Recognize the importance of continuous learning in technical analysis. Stay updated on emerging chart patterns, indicators, and tools to remain at the forefront of market analysis.

Practical Application Through Simulations

- Engage in practical simulations that simulate real market conditions. Apply technical analysis techniques to real-time data and refine your skills through hands-on experience.

Mastery of Technical Analysis

As we conclude this chapter, remember that technical analysis is a dynamic and evolving field. By mastering the tools and techniques presented, you can enhance your ability to make informed decisions, predict market trends, and navigate the complexities of the Indian share market with confidence. In the upcoming chapters, we'll explore strategies for risk management, delve into the psychology of investing, and provide a holistic approach to financial success. Get ready to elevate your investment journey!

Chapter 12: Beyond the Basics - Advanced Trading

Welcome to the realm where seasoned investors thrive - advanced trading strategies. In this chapter, we'll push the boundaries of conventional wisdom, exploring sophisticated techniques and tactics that go beyond the basics, ensuring you're well-equipped to navigate the intricacies of the Indian share market.

Algorithmic Trading and High-Frequency Trading

Delve into the world of algorithmic trading and high-frequency trading (HFT). Understand how computer algorithms execute trades at lightning speed, and explore the opportunities and risks associated with these advanced trading strategies.

Quantitative Trading Strategies

Explore quantitative trading strategies that leverage mathematical models and statistical analysis. From mean reversion to momentum strategies, we'll guide you through quantitative approaches to identify profitable trading opportunities.

Arbitrage Opportunities in the Market

Uncover arbitrage opportunities that arise from price disparities in different markets or financial instruments. Learn how to capitalize on these discrepancies, whether through spatial arbitrage, temporal arbitrage, or statistical arbitrage.

Options and Futures Trading Strategies

Build on your knowledge of options and futures trading with advanced strategies. From complex options spreads to futures spread trading, we'll explore techniques that sophisticated investors use to enhance returns and manage risk.

Pair Trading and Statistical Arbitrage

Dive into pair trading strategies and statistical arbitrage, where traders exploit relationships between different securities. Understand how correlation analysis and quantitative models can be used to identify pairs with potential for profit.

Advanced Technical Analysis

Master advanced technical analysis techniques to refine your market timing and trading decisions. Explore Fibonacci retracements, Elliott Wave theory, and Gann analysis, gaining insights into the more nuanced aspects of technical analysis.

Derivatives Hedging Strategies

Delve into derivatives hedging strategies to protect your portfolio from market volatility. Learn how to use options and futures contracts to hedge against adverse price movements and mitigate risk.

Sector Rotation Models

Refine your sector rotation strategies with advanced models. Explore quantitative approaches to sector analysis, identifying optimal times to rotate in and out of different sectors based on historical performance and economic indicators.

Machine Learning in Trading

Explore the intersection of finance and technology with machine learning in trading. Understand how machine learning algorithms can analyze vast amounts of data to uncover patterns and inform trading decisions.

Dark Pools and Alternative Trading Systems

Gain insights into dark pools and alternative trading systems (ATS). Understand how institutional investors execute large trades away from public exchanges, and explore the advantages and risks associated with these alternative trading venues.

Global Macro Trading

Expand your horizons with global macro trading strategies. Learn how to analyze global economic trends, geopolitical events, and macroeconomic indicators to make informed trading decisions across international markets.

Tax-Efficient Trading Strategies

Explore tax-efficient trading strategies to optimize your investment returns. Learn how to minimize capital gains taxes, take advantage of tax-loss harvesting, and structure your trades to enhance after-tax returns.

Ethical Considerations in Advanced Trading

As we conclude this chapter, we'll address the ethical considerations in advanced trading. Explore the importance of ethical decision-making, transparency, and responsible trading practices to ensure the sustainability of your success in the Indian share market. Stay tuned as we continue to unravel the layers of advanced trading in the upcoming chapters.

Chapter 13: Technical Analysis Demystified

Welcome to the world of charts, patterns, and indicators - technical analysis demystified. In this chapter, we'll unravel the complexities of technical analysis, empowering you to make informed trading decisions based on the art and science of chart interpretation.

Understanding Chart Patterns

Dive into the visual language of technical analysis through chart patterns. Explore classic patterns like head and shoulders, double tops and bottoms, and triangles. Grasp the significance of these patterns in predicting future price movements.

Candlestick Charting Mastery

Master the art of candlestick charting, a powerful tool in technical analysis. Learn to interpret candlestick patterns, recognize bullish and bearish signals, and use candlestick charts to enhance your timing and decision-making.

Moving Averages and Trend Analysis

Explore the role of moving averages in trend analysis. From simple moving averages to exponential moving averages, understand how these indicators smooth price data and provide insights into the direction of market trends.

Oscillators and Momentum Indicators

Delve into oscillators and momentum indicators that help identify overbought and oversold conditions in the market. From Relative Strength Index (RSI) to Stochastic Oscillator, learn how to spot potential trend reversals and confirm existing trends.

Fibonacci Retracement and Extension

Unlock the secrets of Fibonacci retracement and extension levels. Understand how these mathematical ratios can be applied to identify potential support and resistance levels, aiding in precise entry and exit points.

Elliott Wave Theory Decoded

Navigate the complexities of Elliott Wave Theory, a method for understanding market cycles and wave patterns. Learn how to identify and interpret waves, applying this theory to forecast future price movements.

Gann Analysis Techniques

Master Gann analysis techniques, a unique approach that combines geometry and mathematics to analyze price movements. Explore Gann angles, squares, and cycles to enhance your understanding of market trends.

Volume Analysis Strategies

Delve into volume analysis and its role in confirming price trends. Understand how changes in trading volume can provide valuable insights into the strength or weakness of a price movement.

Trendlines and Channels

Explore the use of trendlines and channels in technical analysis. Learn how to draw trendlines accurately, identify trend channels, and use these tools to visualize and interpret market trends.

Point and Figure Charting

Uncover the simplicity and effectiveness of point and figure charting. Explore how this age-old technique filters out market noise, emphasizing significant price movements and aiding in trend identification.

Ichimoku Cloud Analysis

Dive into the world of Ichimoku Cloud analysis, a comprehensive indicator that provides insights into trend direction, support and resistance levels, and potential entry and exit points.

Practical Application of Technical Analysis

As we conclude this chapter, we'll focus on the practical application of technical analysis. Explore real-world examples, case studies, and scenarios where technical analysis has been successfully applied. Armed with this knowledge, you're now equipped to incorporate technical analysis into your trading strategy, gaining a deeper understanding of market movements and trends. Stay tuned for the upcoming chapters where we explore fundamental analysis, options and futures trading, and the psychology of trading.

Chapter 14: Options and Futures Trading Strategies

Welcome to the dynamic world of derivatives -

options and futures trading strategies. In this chapter, we'll explore advanced techniques that

leverage these powerful financial instruments, providing you with the tools to enhance returns and

manage risk in the Indian share market.

Options Trading Strategies

Covered Call Strategy
- Learn how to generate additional income by writing covered calls against your existing stock positions, enhancing your overall returns.

Protective Put Strategy
- Explore the protective put strategy, a risk management technique that involves buying put options to hedge against potential losses in your stock portfolio.

Iron Condor and Butterfly Spreads
- Dive into advanced options spreads like the iron condor and butterfly, strategies that capitalize on market range-bound conditions while managing risk.

Straddle and Strangle Strategies
- Uncover the straddle and strangle strategies, designed to profit from significant price movements, regardless of whether the market goes up or down.

Collar Strategy
- Master the collar strategy, a combination of covered calls and protective puts, providing a balanced approach to risk and return.

Futures Trading Strategies

Trend Following with Futures Contracts
- Understand how trend-following strategies with futures contracts can help you capitalize on sustained market trends.

Pairs Trading with Futures
- Dive into pairs trading using futures contracts, a strategy that involves simultaneously taking long and short positions in correlated assets to benefit from relative price movements.

Hedging with Futures
- Explore how to use futures contracts for hedging purposes, protecting your portfolio from adverse market movements.

Calendar Spread Strategies
- Delve into calendar spread strategies, where futures contracts with different expiration dates are used to capitalize on time decay and market volatility.

Commodity Futures Trading
- Understand the unique aspects of trading commodity futures, including factors such as seasonality, supply and demand dynamics, and geopolitical influences.

Combining Options and Futures Strategies

Synthetic Positions
- Explore the concept of synthetic positions, where options and futures contracts are combined to replicate the payoff of another financial instrument.

Risk Reversal Strategy
- Learn how to implement a risk reversal strategy, combining options to create a position that benefits from both upward and downward price movements.

Delta Hedging
- Understand delta hedging as a risk management technique, involving the use of options to offset the directional risk of an underlying asset.

Advanced Options and Futures Trading Tips

Implied Volatility Strategies
- Explore strategies that capitalize on changes in implied volatility, a key factor in options pricing.

Options Greeks and Their Practical Use
- Delve into the practical application of options Greeks (Delta, Gamma, Theta, Vega) and how they can guide your options trading decisions.

Futures Spread Trading
- Understand futures spread trading strategies, where positions in different futures contracts are taken to benefit from price differentials.

Risk Management in Derivatives Trading

As we conclude this chapter, we'll emphasize the importance of risk management in derivatives trading. Learn how to use options and futures strategically to hedge against potential losses and safeguard your portfolio. Armed with a comprehensive understanding of these advanced trading strategies, you're well-prepared to navigate the derivatives landscape in the Indian share market. Stay tuned for the next chapters where we explore risk management strategies, the psychology of trading, and more.

Chapter 15: Risk Management Strategies

Safeguarding Your Investments in the Market Jungle

In the unpredictable jungle of the stock market, mastering risk management is the key to preserving your capital and navigating the terrain with confidence. In this chapter, we'll explore various risk management strategies to shield your investments from potential pitfalls.

Understanding Investment Risks

Identifying Market Risks
- Dive into the different types of market risks, including systematic and unsystematic risks. Understanding these risks is crucial for developing effective risk management strategies.

Company-Specific Risks
- Explore risks specific to individual companies, such as management changes, industry trends, and competitive pressures. Recognizing company-specific risks is essential for making informed investment decisions.

Diversification Strategies

Portfolio Diversification
- Master the art of portfolio diversification. Learn how spreading your investments across various asset classes, sectors, and geographic regions can reduce the impact of adverse market movements.

Risk-Adjusted Returns

- Understand the concept of risk-adjusted returns. Evaluate investments not only based on potential returns but also on the level of risk involved, ensuring a balanced risk-reward profile.

Hedging Techniques

Options and Futures
- Explore the use of options and futures as hedging tools. Learn how these financial instruments can help you protect your portfolio from adverse market movements.

Inverse Exchange-Traded Funds (ETFs)
- Understand the role of inverse ETFs in hedging. These funds aim to provide returns opposite to the benchmark index, offering a way to profit during market downturns.

Stop-Loss Orders and Limit Orders

Implementing Stop-Loss Orders
- Embrace the use of stop-loss orders to limit potential losses. These orders automatically sell a security when it reaches a predetermined price, protecting your investment from significant declines.

Setting Limit Orders
- Explore the benefits of setting limit orders. By specifying the maximum or minimum price at which you are willing to buy or sell, you can control the execution price of your trades.

Stress Testing Your Portfolio

Simulating Market Scenarios
- Engage in stress testing for your portfolio. Simulate various market scenarios to assess how your investments may perform under adverse conditions, helping you identify vulnerabilities.

Scenario Analysis for Risk Assessment
- Conduct scenario analysis to assess potential risks. Evaluate how changes in economic conditions, interest rates, or geopolitical events could impact your portfolio.

Continuous Monitoring and Adjustments

Regular Portfolio Reviews
- Make regular reviews of your portfolio a habit. Stay vigilant to changes in market conditions, economic trends, and company-specific factors that may necessitate adjustments to your risk management strategies.

Adapting to Dynamic Markets

- Embrace adaptability in dynamic markets. Recognize that risk management is an ongoing process that requires adjustments as market conditions evolve.

Setting Risk Tolerance and Position Sizing

Risk Tolerance Assessment
- Understand how to assess your risk tolerance, considering factors such as financial goals, time horizon, and emotional resilience.

Position Sizing Techniques
- Explore various position sizing methods, including fixed fractional position sizing and the Kelly Criterion, to optimize the allocation of capital to different trades.

Stop-Loss and Take-Profit Strategies

Setting Effective Stop-Loss Orders
- Master the art of setting effective stop-loss orders to limit potential losses and protect your portfolio from adverse market movements.

Implementing Take-Profit Orders
- Explore strategies for implementing take-profit orders to lock in gains and ensure disciplined profit-taking in line with your trading plan.

Diversification and Asset Allocation

Benefits of Diversification
- Understand the benefits of diversification in spreading risk across different assets, sectors, and geographies.

Strategic Asset Allocation
- Explore strategic asset allocation strategies based on your investment goals, risk tolerance, and market outlook.

Risk-Adjusted Returns and Sharpe Ratio

Understanding Risk-Adjusted Returns
- Learn how to assess the performance of your investments in relation to the level of risk taken, focusing on risk-adjusted returns.

Calculating the Sharpe Ratio
- Dive into the calculation and interpretation of the Sharpe Ratio, a key metric for evaluating the risk-adjusted performance of an investment or portfolio.

Stress Testing and Scenario Analysis

Stress Testing Your Portfolio

- Explore stress testing methodologies to evaluate how your portfolio may perform under extreme market conditions.

Scenario Analysis for Contingency Planning
- Learn how to conduct scenario analysis to anticipate and prepare for various market scenarios, enhancing your ability to respond to unexpected events.

Options as Risk Management Tools

Protective Put Options
- Understand how protective put options can serve as insurance against potential declines in the value of your stock portfolio.

Covered Call Strategies for Income Generation
- Explore covered call strategies as a means of generating additional income while potentially offsetting losses.

Monitoring and Adjusting Risk Management Strategies

Regular Portfolio Reviews
- Emphasize the importance of regular portfolio reviews to assess the ongoing effectiveness of your risk management strategies.

Dynamic Adjustments
- Learn how to dynamically adjust your risk management strategies based on changes in market conditions, volatility, and your financial goals.

Behavioral Aspects of Risk Management

Emotional Discipline and Decision-Making
- Understand the behavioral aspects of risk management, focusing on emotional discipline, and making rational decisions during periods of market uncertainty.

Learning from Mistakes
- Embrace a culture of learning from mistakes, understanding that setbacks are inherent in trading and investing, and using them as opportunities for improvement.

The Holistic Approach to Risk Management

As we conclude this chapter, we stress the importance of adopting a holistic approach to risk management. By integrating diverse strategies and techniques, you can fortify your financial journey, minimize downside risks, and create a resilient portfolio. Stay tuned for the upcoming chapters where we explore the psychology of trading, market analysis techniques, and more.

Risk Management as a Strategic Imperative

As we conclude this chapter, remember that risk management is not just a defensive strategy but a strategic imperative. By incorporating diverse risk management tools and techniques, you can navigate the uncertainties of the market while safeguarding your investments. In the next chapters, we'll delve into the psychology of investing and explore advanced strategies for sustained financial success. Get ready to fortify your journey through the Indian share market!

Chapter 16: Investment Psychology - Mastering Your Mind

The Mental Game of Investing

Welcome to the intricate world of investment psychology, where emotions, biases, and cognitive processes play a pivotal role in decision-making. In this chapter, we'll delve into the psychological aspects of investing and explore strategies to master your mind in the face of market fluctuations.

Emotions in Investing

The Impact of Fear and Greed
- Uncover the powerful impact of emotions like fear and greed on investment decisions. Understanding how these emotions influence behavior is crucial for maintaining a rational and disciplined approach.

Overcoming Emotional Biases

- Explore common emotional biases that can cloud judgment, such as loss aversion, confirmation bias, and herd mentality. Learn strategies to recognize and overcome these biases in your decision-making process.

Discipline and Patience

Setting Clear Investment Goals
- Establish clear and realistic investment goals. Having a well-defined roadmap provides a sense of purpose, helping you stay disciplined in your investment approach.

Maintaining Patience During Volatility
- Cultivate patience, especially during periods of market volatility. Understand that investing is a long-term journey, and short-term fluctuations should not derail your overall strategy.

Psychological Resilience

Learning from Setbacks
- Embrace setbacks as opportunities for learning and growth. Analyze investment decisions, understand the factors influencing outcomes, and use this knowledge to improve future strategies.

Building Emotional Resilience
- Build emotional resilience to withstand market uncertainties. Develop a mindset that can navigate both favorable and challenging market conditions without succumbing to emotional extremes.

Rational Decision-Making

Data-Driven Decision-Making
- Prioritize data-driven decision-making. Base your choices on thorough research, analysis, and a rational assessment of risks and rewards rather than succumbing to impulsive actions.

The Importance of Continuous Learning
- Engage in continuous learning to enhance your investment knowledge. The more informed you are, the more confident and rational your investment decisions will be.

Behavioral Finance Strategies

Applying Behavioral Finance Principles
- Apply principles from behavioral finance to your investment approach. Utilize strategies such as setting pre-determined exit points, maintaining a diversified portfolio, and staying informed to counteract emotional biases.

Seeking Professional Guidance

- Consider seeking professional guidance from financial advisors. A trusted advisor can provide objective insights, helping you navigate emotional challenges and make well-informed decisions.

Psychological Self-Awareness

Regular Self-Reflection
- Engage in regular self-reflection to enhance psychological self-awareness. Understand your own risk tolerance, biases, and emotional triggers to make conscious and informed investment choices.

Mindfulness and Stress Reduction
- Incorporate mindfulness and stress reduction techniques into your routine. Managing stress and maintaining a calm mindset are essential for making clear-headed investment decisions.

The Harmonious Mindset

As we conclude this chapter, remember that mastering investment psychology is an ongoing journey. By fostering discipline, patience, and psychological resilience, you can create a harmonious mindset that empowers you to make confident and rational decisions, irrespective of market conditions. In the following chapters, we'll explore advanced portfolio management strategies and delve into the evolving landscape of technological innovations in the Indian share market. Get ready to elevate your investment journey!

Chapter 17: The Psychology of Trading

Welcome to the intriguing intersection of human psychology and financial markets. In this chapter, we'll explore the psychological aspects of trading, helping you understand and navigate the emotions, biases, and mental challenges that influence decision-making in the Indian share market.

Emotions in Trading

Greed and Fear
- Recognize the impact of greed and fear on trading decisions, understanding how these emotions can drive impulsive actions and hinder rational judgment.

Patience and Impatience
- Explore the importance of patience in trading, recognizing the potential pitfalls of impatience and the value of waiting for optimal market conditions.

Overcoming Loss Aversion
- Understand loss aversion, the tendency to prefer avoiding losses over acquiring equivalent gains, and learn techniques to overcome this cognitive bias.

Cognitive Biases in Trading

Confirmation Bias

- Recognize the influence of confirmation bias, where individuals seek information that confirms their pre-existing beliefs, and learn strategies to mitigate its impact on trading decisions.

Herd Mentality
- Explore the herd mentality in financial markets, understanding the risks of blindly following the crowd, and developing an independent mindset.

Anchoring Bias
- Understand anchoring bias, the tendency to rely too heavily on the first piece of information encountered, and learn how to make unbiased assessments in trading.

Discipline and Consistency

Trading Plan Adherence
- Emphasize the importance of adhering to your trading plan, maintaining discipline, and avoiding impulsive decisions that deviate from your predefined strategy.

Consistent Risk Management
- Recognize the role of consistent risk management in maintaining stability and protecting your capital, even in the face of emotional highs and lows.

Dealing with Trading Stress

Meditation and Mindfulness
- Explore mindfulness and meditation techniques to manage stress, enhance focus, and maintain a clear mindset during periods of market volatility.

Physical Exercise for Mental Well-being
- Understand the connection between physical exercise and mental well-being, incorporating a healthy lifestyle to support optimal trading performance.

Learning from Mistakes and Adaptation

Post-Trade Analysis
- Embrace post-trade analysis as a tool for learning from mistakes, identifying areas of improvement, and continuously evolving as a trader.

Adaptability to Market Changes
- Develop adaptability to market changes, recognizing that flexibility and the ability to adjust strategies are essential for long-term success.

Developing a Trader's Mindset

Risk-Taking and Risk Management Balance
- Strike a balance between risk-taking and risk management, cultivating a mindset that values calculated decisions over impulsive actions.

Focus on Process, Not Just Outcomes

- Shift your focus from outcomes to the process, understanding that consistent, well-executed strategies lead to success in the long run.

Seeking Professional Guidance

Mental Health and Trading
- Acknowledge the importance of mental health in trading and consider seeking professional guidance when psychological challenges impact your well-being.

Trading Communities and Support Networks
- Engage with trading communities and support networks to share experiences, gain insights, and foster a sense of camaraderie in the trading journey.

Balancing Rationality and Intuition

As we conclude this chapter, recognize the delicate balance between rationality and intuition in trading. While a logical approach is crucial, intuition can be a valuable guide when supported by experience and knowledge. Stay tuned for the upcoming chapters where we explore market analysis techniques, investment strategies, and more.

Chapter 18: Market Analysis Techniques

Welcome to the heart of informed decision-making –

market analysis techniques. In this chapter, we'll explore a range of analytical tools and methodologies that empower you to interpret market trends, identify opportunities, and make strategic moves in the Indian share market.

Fundamental Analysis Refresher

Economic Indicators
- Delve deeper into economic indicators and their impact on the stock market. Understand how factors such as GDP growth, inflation rates, and employment figures influence market sentiment.

Industry and Sector Analysis
- Expand your sector analysis skills, examining industry trends, competitive landscapes, and external factors that can shape the performance of specific sectors.

Technical Analysis Evolution

Advanced Chart Patterns
- Explore advanced chart patterns, combining multiple signals for a more nuanced understanding of market movements. Patterns like cup and handle, flags, and wedges can offer valuable insights.

Volume Price Analysis
- Dive into volume price analysis to assess the strength of price movements. Learn how trading volume can validate or invalidate price trends, providing a more comprehensive view of market dynamics.

Sentiment Analysis and News Trading

Sentiment Indicators
- Understand sentiment indicators, gauging the mood of market participants. From the CBOE Volatility Index (VIX) to put/call ratios, explore tools that reflect market sentiment.

News Trading Strategies
- Explore news trading strategies, leveraging breaking news and economic events to make timely and informed trading decisions. Learn how to interpret news releases and their potential impact on the market.

Quantitative Analysis in Trading

Algorithmic Trading Strategies
- Delve into algorithmic trading strategies, where mathematical models and algorithms automate trading decisions. Understand the advantages and risks associated with algorithmic trading.

Machine Learning Applications
- Explore the applications of machine learning in market analysis. From predicting price movements to identifying patterns, machine learning can provide valuable insights for traders.

Combining Fundamental and Technical Analysis

Confluence Analysis
- Master confluence analysis, a technique that combines both fundamental and technical analysis to validate trading signals. Learn how aligning different indicators can strengthen your decision-making process.

Top-Down vs. Bottom-Up Analysis
- Explore the top-down and bottom-up approaches to market analysis. Understand how starting with a broad economic perspective and narrowing down to individual stocks can enhance your overall analysis.

Behavioral Analysis and Market Psychology

Market Profile Analysis
- Dive into market profile analysis, a tool that visualizes price and volume data to identify areas of support and resistance. Understand how market profile can offer insights into market psychology.

Tick and Time Charts
- Explore tick and time charts as alternatives to traditional candlestick charts. Learn how these charts provide a different perspective on price movements, focusing on transaction volume and time intervals.

Real-Time Data and Advanced Analytics

Utilizing Real-Time Data
- Emphasize the importance of real-time data in market analysis. Learn how to access and interpret live market data to make timely decisions.

Big Data Analytics in Finance
- Understand the role of big data analytics in financial markets. Explore how processing vast amounts of data can uncover patterns, trends, and correlations that inform trading strategies.

Intermarket Analysis

Intermarket Relationships
- Explore intermarket analysis, examining the relationships between different asset classes. Understand how movements in currencies, commodities, and bonds can influence stock markets.

Correlation and Divergence Analysis
- Learn how to analyze correlations and divergences between different assets. Identify patterns that indicate potential market trends or reversals.

Customizing Your Analytical Toolkit

As we conclude this chapter, recognize the importance of customizing your analytical toolkit. Every trader is unique, and tailoring your approach with a combination of these techniques can provide a more holistic view of the market. Stay tuned for the upcoming chapters where we explore investment strategies, portfolio management, and more.

Chapter 19: Portfolio Management Strategies for Success

Crafting a Winning Portfolio

In this chapter, we'll delve into the art and science of portfolio management – the process of constructing and adjusting your investment portfolio to align with your financial goals, risk tolerance, and market conditions. Mastering portfolio management is essential for achieving sustained success in the Indian share market.

Defining Your Investment Objectives

Short-Term vs. Long-Term Goals
- Clearly define your investment objectives, distinguishing between short-term and long-term goals. Tailor your portfolio strategy to the time horizon of your financial aspirations.

Risk Tolerance Assessment

- Assess your risk tolerance objectively. Understand how much volatility and market fluctuations you can comfortably endure without compromising your financial well-being.

Building a Diversified Portfolio

Asset Allocation Strategies
- Explore various asset allocation strategies based on your risk tolerance and financial goals. Allocate your investments among different asset classes, such as equities, fixed income, and alternative investments, to diversify risk.

Sector and Industry Diversification
- Dive into sector and industry diversification within your equity holdings. Avoid overexposure to a specific sector and spread your investments to minimize the impact of adverse developments in any single industry.

Active vs. Passive Investing

Understanding Active Management
- Delve into the concept of active portfolio management. Understand how actively managed funds aim to outperform the market through strategic stock selection and timing.

Benefits of Passive Investing
- Explore the benefits of passive investing through index funds and exchange-traded funds (ETFs). Passive strategies aim to replicate the performance of a market index, providing diversification at lower costs.

Tactical Portfolio Adjustments

Rebalancing Strategies
- Implement regular portfolio rebalancing. Adjust your asset allocation periodically to maintain your desired risk-return profile and capitalize on market opportunities.

Tax-Efficient Strategies
- Consider tax-efficient portfolio management strategies. Optimize your investment decisions to minimize tax implications, such as capital gains, and enhance after-tax returns.

Value Investing and Growth Strategies

Value Investing Principles
- Embrace the principles of value investing. Identify undervalued stocks with strong fundamentals, aiming for long-term capital appreciation.

Growth Investing Strategies

- Explore growth investing strategies. Identify companies with high growth potential, often reinvesting profits for expansion, with the aim of achieving capital appreciation over time.

Sustainable Investing

ESG Integration
- Incorporate Environmental, Social, and Governance (ESG) principles into your investment strategy. Align your portfolio with companies demonstrating strong ethical and sustainable practices.

Impact Investing
- Explore impact investing opportunities. Direct your investments toward companies and projects that aim to generate positive social and environmental impacts alongside financial returns.

Regular Monitoring and Review

Performance Evaluation
- Regularly evaluate the performance of your portfolio. Assess the achievement of your investment objectives and make adjustments based on evolving market conditions and personal financial goals.

Adapting to Market Changes
- Stay agile and adapt to market changes. Continuously reassess your portfolio in response to economic trends, geopolitical events, and emerging opportunities or risks.

The Road to Financial Success

As we conclude this chapter, remember that portfolio management is a dynamic and personalized process. By aligning your investments with your objectives, regularly reassessing your strategy, and adapting to market conditions, you pave the way for financial success in the Indian share market. In the subsequent chapters, we'll explore the evolving landscape of technological innovations and delve into sustainable investing practices. Get ready to elevate your portfolio management skills!

Chapter 20: Investment Strategies for Success

Welcome to the strategic realm of investment –

where decisions are not just about trades, but about building a robust, diversified portfolio for long-term success in the Indian share market. In this chapter, we'll explore various investment strategies that align with different risk profiles and financial goals.

Long-Term Investing Strategies

Buy and Hold Strategy
- Embrace the simplicity of the buy and hold strategy, where investors purchase quality stocks and hold them for an extended period. Explore the advantages and considerations of this long-term approach.

Dividend Growth Investing
- Dive into dividend growth investing, a strategy focused on selecting stocks with a history of consistent dividend increases. Discover how this approach combines income generation with capital appreciation.

Value Investing Principles

Benjamin Graham's Value Investing
- Understand the foundational principles of value investing introduced by Benjamin Graham, including the importance of intrinsic value, margin of safety, and thorough financial analysis.

Warren Buffett's Approach
- Explore Warren Buffett's investment philosophy, emphasizing the concept of buying wonderful companies at fair prices. Learn how to apply Buffett's principles to identify sustainable, high-quality investments.

Growth Investing Strategies

Peter Lynch's Growth Investing
- Delve into growth investing strategies inspired by Peter Lynch, focusing on identifying companies with strong earnings growth potential. Learn how to spot promising growth stocks early in their trajectory.

CAN SLIM Methodology
- Explore the CAN SLIM methodology developed by William J. O'Neil. This strategy combines technical and fundamental analysis to identify stocks with both growth potential and momentum.

Momentum Investing Techniques

Trend Following Strategies
- Embrace trend following strategies, where investors ride existing market trends to maximize profits. Understand the importance of identifying and participating in prevailing market momentum.

Relative Strength Investing
- Explore relative strength investing, a strategy that involves selecting assets that have outperformed their peers. Learn how to use relative strength indicators to identify strong-performing investments.

Contrarian Investing Approaches

Contrarian Investing Principles
- Understand the principles of contrarian investing, where investors actively seek opportunities in assets that are currently out of favor. Learn how to navigate market sentiment and capitalize on market mispricing.

Value Averaging Strategy
- Dive into the value averaging strategy, a contrarian approach where investors adjust their investment amounts based on the performance of their portfolio. Explore how this strategy maintains discipline in varying market conditions.

Tactical Asset Allocation

Strategic vs. Tactical Asset Allocation
- Explore the differences between strategic and tactical asset allocation. Understand how tactical asset allocation involves actively adjusting your portfolio based on short-term market conditions.

Dynamic Portfolio Rebalancing
- Master dynamic portfolio rebalancing, a strategy that involves periodically adjusting the allocation of assets in your portfolio to maintain the desired risk and return profile.

Risk Parity and All-Weather Strategies

Risk Parity Investing
- Understand risk parity investing, a strategy that seeks to balance risk across different asset classes. Explore how this approach aims to enhance portfolio stability in varying market conditions.

All-Weather Portfolio Strategy
- Explore the all-weather portfolio strategy, popularized by Ray Dalio. Learn how this balanced portfolio is designed to perform well in all economic environments, providing stability and consistent returns.

ESG (Environmental, Social, and Governance) Investing

Principles of ESG Investing
- Delve into the principles of ESG investing, where environmental, social, and governance factors are integrated into the investment decision-making process. Understand how this approach aligns investments with ethical and sustainability considerations.

Impact Investing
- Explore impact investing, a strategy where investors actively seek opportunities that generate positive social or environmental outcomes alongside financial returns. Learn how impact investing contributes to positive change.

Systematic Investment Plans (SIPs) and Dollar-Cost Averaging

SIPs in Mutual Funds
- Understand systematic investment plans (SIPs) in mutual funds, a disciplined approach to regular investing. Explore how SIPs allow investors to accumulate units over time, regardless of market fluctuations.

Dollar-Cost Averaging
- Master dollar-cost averaging, a strategy where investors consistently invest a fixed amount, buying more shares when prices are low and fewer when prices are high. Explore how this approach reduces the impact of market volatility.

Customizing Your Investment Approach

As we conclude this chapter, recognize the importance of customizing your investment approach. Depending on your financial goals, risk tolerance, and time horizon, you may choose to adopt a combination of these strategies. Stay tuned for the upcoming chapters where we explore portfolio management, investment psychology, and more.

Chapter 21: Portfolio Management Strategies

Welcome to the realm where investment strategies converge into a comprehensive portfolio. In this chapter, we'll explore various portfolio management strategies that focus on balancing risk, diversification, and optimizing returns for sustained success in the Indian share market.

Modern Portfolio Theory (MPT)

Asset Allocation Principles
- Understand the principles of asset allocation, a cornerstone of Modern Portfolio Theory. Explore how diversifying investments across different asset classes can enhance risk-adjusted returns.

Efficient Frontier Analysis
- Dive into efficient frontier analysis, a tool used in MPT to identify portfolios that offer the maximum expected return for a given level of risk or the minimum risk for a given level of return.

Risk-Return Optimization Techniques

Sharpe Ratio and Risk-Adjusted Returns
- Master the Sharpe Ratio, a key measure of risk-adjusted returns. Explore how this metric guides investors in balancing the trade-off between risk and return in their portfolios.

Treynor Ratio for Systematic Risk Assessment
- Understand the Treynor Ratio, which evaluates the efficiency of a portfolio in relation to its systematic risk. Learn how this ratio aids in assessing the returns earned per unit of systematic risk taken.

Factor Investing and Smart Beta

Understanding Factor Investing
- Delve into factor investing, where portfolios are constructed based on specific factors like value, size, momentum, and quality. Explore how these factors can influence portfolio performance.

Implementing Smart Beta Strategies
- Explore smart beta strategies, which aim to capture specific factors believed to contribute to outperformance. Understand how smart beta ETFs and funds apply factor-based approaches.

Tactical Asset Allocation (TAA)

Dynamic Portfolio Adjustments
- Understand the dynamics of tactical asset allocation, where portfolio weights are actively adjusted based on short-term market conditions. Explore how TAA responds to changing market environments.

Market Timing Considerations
- Explore the challenges and considerations associated with market timing in tactical asset allocation. Understand how disciplined and well-researched decisions can contribute to portfolio success.

Global Diversification and Emerging Markets

Benefits of Global Diversification
- Embrace the benefits of global diversification, spreading investments across different regions to reduce risk and capitalize on diverse market opportunities.

Investing in Emerging Markets
- Delve into the unique considerations of investing in emerging markets. Understand the potential rewards and risks associated with including emerging market assets in your portfolio.

Tail Risk Hedging Strategies

Options and Derivatives for Hedging
- Explore the use of options and derivatives for tail risk hedging. Understand how these instruments can provide insurance against extreme market events.

Protective Put Strategies
- Dive into protective put strategies as a form of tail risk hedging. Learn how purchasing put options can safeguard your portfolio from significant declines.

Long-Short Strategies and Market Neutral Funds

Long-Short Equity Strategies
- Understand long-short equity strategies, where investors simultaneously take long positions in promising stocks and short positions in weaker ones. Explore how this approach aims to generate returns regardless of market direction.

Market Neutral Funds
- Explore market neutral funds, which seek to achieve returns independent of overall market movements. Understand how these funds balance long and short positions to minimize market exposure.

Real Assets and Alternative Investments

Incorporating Real Assets
- Delve into the inclusion of real assets like real estate, commodities, and infrastructure in your portfolio. Explore how these assets can provide diversification benefits.

Venture Capital and Private Equity Exposure
- Explore the potential benefits and considerations of including venture capital and private equity investments in your portfolio. Understand the illiquidity and potential returns associated with these alternative assets.

Robo-Advisors and Algorithmic Portfolio Management

Automated Portfolio Management
- Understand the role of robo-advisors in automating portfolio management. Explore how algorithms analyze investor profiles and market conditions to create and rebalance portfolios.

Algorithmic Trading for Portfolio Adjustments
- Delve into algorithmic trading strategies for portfolio adjustments. Learn how algorithms can respond to market signals, optimizing portfolio composition based on predefined rules.

Environmental, Social, and Governance (ESG) Integration

ESG Considerations in Portfolio Construction

- Embrace ESG integration in portfolio construction. Understand how environmental, social, and governance factors can guide investment decisions aligned with ethical and sustainable principles.

Impact Investing in Portfolios

- Explore the incorporation of impact investing in portfolios. Understand how portfolios can be designed to align with specific social or environmental goals, contributing to positive change.

Customizing Your Portfolio Management Approach

As we conclude this chapter, recognize the importance of customizing your portfolio management approach. Tailor your strategy to align with your risk tolerance, investment goals, and time horizon. Stay tuned for the upcoming chapters where we explore investment psychology, risk management, and the evolving landscape of the Indian share market.

Chapter 22: The Evolving Landscape - Technological Innovations

Navigating the Future: Technology in Indian Share Market

In this chapter, we embark on a journey into the evolving landscape of the Indian share market, where technological innovations shape the way investors analyze, trade, and interact with financial markets. Understanding these innovations is essential for staying ahead in an increasingly digital and dynamic environment.

Artificial Intelligence and Machine Learning

AI-Driven Analytics
- Explore the impact of Artificial Intelligence (AI) on market analysis. AI-driven analytics leverage machine learning algorithms to process vast amounts of data, providing insights into market trends and investment opportunities.

Algorithmic Trading
- Delve into algorithmic trading powered by machine learning. Algorithms execute trades based on predefined criteria, optimizing entry and exit points and reacting to market conditions at speeds beyond human capability.

Blockchain and Cryptocurrencies

Decentralized Ledger Technology (DLT)
- Understand the concept of Blockchain and its application in the financial sector. Blockchain, as a decentralized ledger, enhances transparency and security in transactions.

Cryptocurrencies as Alternative Investments
- Explore the emergence of cryptocurrencies as alternative investments. Learn how digital assets like Bitcoin and Ethereum provide new avenues for diversification within investment portfolios.

Robo-Advisors and Fintech Platforms

Automated Financial Advisory Services
- Embrace the rise of Robo-Advisors. These automated platforms utilize algorithms to provide personalized investment advice and portfolio management tailored to individual investor profiles.

Fintech Innovations
- Explore broader Fintech innovations transforming financial services. From payment systems to peer-to-peer lending, Fintech platforms revolutionize how individuals access and manage their finances.

Big Data Analytics

Harnessing Big Data for Market Insights
- Dive into the realm of Big Data analytics in finance. Discover how vast datasets are processed and analyzed to extract actionable insights, enabling investors to make more informed decisions.

Predictive Analytics for Market Trends
- Explore predictive analytics applications in forecasting market trends. By analyzing historical data and patterns, predictive analytics aids in anticipating potential market movements.

Cybersecurity in Financial Markets

Securing Financial Transactions
- Understand the critical role of cybersecurity in financial markets. As technology advances, ensuring the security of financial transactions and protecting sensitive information becomes paramount.

Blockchain for Enhanced Security
- Explore how Blockchain enhances cybersecurity in financial transactions. Its decentralized nature reduces the risk of fraudulent activities, providing a secure foundation for digital transactions.

Mobile Trading and Accessibility

Empowering Investors with Mobile Trading
- Witness the transformation of trading through mobile platforms. Mobile trading apps provide real-time market access, enabling investors to trade and manage portfolios on the go.

Enhancing Accessibility for Retail Investors
- Explore how technological innovations enhance accessibility for retail investors. Lowering entry barriers and providing user-friendly interfaces democratize participation in the share market.

Continuous Learning in Technological Advancements

Adapting to Technological Changes
- Embrace a mindset of continuous learning to adapt to technological changes. Stay informed about emerging technologies and their applications in the financial sector to remain competitive.

Practical Application Through Simulations
- Engage in practical simulations to familiarize yourself with technological advancements. Simulations offer hands-on experience in navigating digital platforms and leveraging technology for investment strategies.

Embracing Technological Innovations

Fintech Revolution
- Explore the impact of the fintech revolution on the Indian share market. Understand how technological innovations in financial services, such as robo-advisors, blockchain, and digital payment systems, are reshaping the industry.

Algorithmic Trading and High-Frequency Trading
- Delve into the world of algorithmic trading and high-frequency trading. Understand how these advanced trading strategies leverage algorithms and computer algorithms to execute trades at lightning speed.

Rise of Artificial Intelligence (AI) in Finance

AI-Powered Investment Strategies
- Explore AI-powered investment strategies that utilize machine learning algorithms to analyze vast datasets and identify market trends. Understand how AI is transforming decision-making processes in finance.

Natural Language Processing (NLP) in Market Analysis
- Dive into the role of natural language processing (NLP) in market analysis. Learn how NLP algorithms process and analyze textual data from news articles, social media, and financial reports to gauge market sentiment.

Cryptocurrencies and Decentralized Finance (DeFi)

Cryptocurrency Landscape
- Understand the evolving landscape of cryptocurrencies in the Indian market. Explore the challenges and opportunities associated with digital currencies like Bitcoin, Ethereum, and the potential for decentralized finance (DeFi) platforms.

DeFi Platforms and Smart Contracts
- Delve into decentralized finance (DeFi) platforms and the role of smart contracts in automating financial transactions. Explore how these technologies are reshaping traditional financial services.

Sustainable and ESG Investing Growth

Rise of Sustainable Investing
- Explore the rise of sustainable investing in the Indian share market. Understand how environmental, social, and governance (ESG) considerations are influencing investment decisions and reshaping corporate practices.

Green Bonds and Social Impact Investments
- Dive into the growing market for green bonds and social impact investments. Learn how these financial instruments contribute to sustainable development and address global challenges.

Evolving Regulatory Landscape

Regulatory Changes in Financial Markets
- Understand the evolving regulatory landscape in Indian financial markets. Explore how regulatory changes impact market participants, shape investment strategies, and contribute to market transparency.

Digital Securities and Regulatory Frameworks
- Delve into the emergence of digital securities and the evolving regulatory frameworks governing these assets. Explore how the digitization of traditional securities is changing the way assets are issued and traded.

Shifting Global Economic Dynamics

Global Economic Trends and India's Positioning
- Explore shifting global economic dynamics and their impact on the Indian share market. Understand how geopolitical events, trade relationships, and economic trends influence investment opportunities.

Globalization and Cross-Border Investments
- Delve into the increasing globalization of financial markets. Explore the opportunities and challenges associated with cross-border investments and the integration of Indian markets into the global economy.

Behavioral Finance in the Digital Age

Online Trading Platforms and Investor Behavior
- Understand how online trading platforms influence investor behavior. Explore the impact of digital interfaces on decision-making, trading patterns, and market participation.

Social Trading and Community Influence
- Dive into the phenomenon of social trading, where investors share and replicate each other's trading strategies. Explore the influence of online communities on investment decisions and market sentiment.

The Future of Trading and Investing

Innovations in Trading Platforms
- Explore the future of trading platforms. Understand how advancements in user interfaces, data analytics, and connectivity are shaping the next generation of trading tools.

Integration of Virtual and Augmented Reality
- Delve into the potential integration of virtual and augmented reality in financial services. Explore how these technologies could enhance data visualization, analytics, and the overall trading experience.

Adapting to Change and Staying Informed

Continuous Learning and Adaptation
- Emphasize the importance of continuous learning in the dynamic landscape of the Indian share market. Explore resources, educational platforms, and strategies for staying informed and adapting to market changes.

Strategic Portfolio Adjustments
- Understand the need for strategic portfolio adjustments in response to evolving market trends. Explore how proactive decision-making can position investors to capitalize on emerging opportunities.

As we conclude this chapter, recognize that navigating the evolving landscape of the Indian share market requires agility, adaptability, and a forward-looking mindset. Stay tuned for the final chapters where we explore investment psychology, risk management, and the holistic approach to financial success.

Embracing the Future

As we conclude this chapter, remember that technological innovations are reshaping the landscape of the Indian share market. By staying informed and embracing these advancements, you position yourself to leverage new opportunities and navigate the evolving financial ecosystem. In the upcoming chapters, we'll explore sustainable investing practices and strategies tailored for different market conditions. Get ready to embrace the future of finance!

Chapter 23: Sustainable Investing - Balancing Profit and Purpose

The Rise of Sustainable and Responsible Investment

In this chapter, we'll explore the transformative impact of sustainable investing, where financial considerations merge with environmental, social, and governance (ESG) principles. Understanding this paradigm shift is crucial for investors seeking to align their portfolios with ethical and sustainable practices.

ESG Integration in Investment Decisions

Environmental Considerations
- Delve into the integration of environmental factors in investment decisions. Evaluate companies based on their ecological footprint, commitment to renewable energy, and environmental sustainability practices.

Social Responsibility Metrics

- Explore the incorporation of social responsibility metrics in investment analysis. Consider factors such as labor practices, diversity and inclusion, and community engagement to assess a company's societal impact.

Governance and Ethical Practices

Emphasizing Strong Governance
- Understand the importance of strong governance in sustainable investing. Companies with transparent governance structures, ethical leadership, and shareholder-friendly practices are often favored.

Ethical Business Practices
- Explore the significance of ethical business practices. Investors increasingly seek companies that uphold high ethical standards, fostering trust and long-term sustainability.

Impact Investing for Positive Change

Aligning Investments with Values
- Embrace impact investing as a strategy to align investments with personal values. Direct capital towards companies and projects that aim to generate positive social and environmental impacts alongside financial returns.

Measuring Social and Environmental Impact
- Understand methodologies for measuring the social and environmental impact of investments. Impact metrics go beyond financial returns, providing a holistic assessment of a portfolio's contributions to positive change.

Sustainable Investment Funds

Sustainable Mutual Funds and ETFs
- Explore the growing landscape of sustainable mutual funds and exchange-traded funds (ETFs). These investment vehicles allow individuals to participate in a diversified portfolio of companies committed to ESG principles.

Performance and Returns
- Address common misconceptions about the performance of sustainable investments. Studies indicate that sustainable funds can deliver competitive returns while aligning with investors' ethical values.

Corporate Transparency and Reporting

The Role of Corporate Reporting
- Recognize the importance of corporate transparency and reporting in sustainable investing. Companies that disclose ESG information enable investors to make informed decisions aligned with their values.

Regulatory Trends in ESG Disclosure
- Stay informed about regulatory trends related to ESG disclosure. Increasingly, regulatory bodies are advocating for standardized reporting, enhancing transparency in the marketplace.

Engaging with Companies on ESG Issues

Shareholder Activism
- Explore the concept of shareholder activism in sustainable investing. Engage with companies on ESG issues through proxy voting, shareholder resolutions, and direct dialogue to drive positive change.

Collaborative Initiatives
- Participate in collaborative initiatives promoting sustainable practices. Investors, NGOs, and businesses can work together to address global challenges and advocate for responsible business conduct.

The Integration of Sustainability in Portfolio Management

Tailoring Portfolios for Sustainable Goals
- Learn how to integrate sustainability into portfolio management. Tailor your investment strategy to align with sustainable goals, considering ESG factors alongside traditional financial metrics.

Sustainability as a Risk Mitigation Strategy
- Recognize sustainability as a risk mitigation strategy. Companies with strong ESG practices may be better equipped to navigate challenges, reducing the overall risk in a portfolio.

Embracing a Sustainable Future

As we conclude this chapter, remember that sustainable investing goes beyond financial returns—it represents a commitment to creating a positive impact on the world. By incorporating ESG principles into your investment strategy, you not only contribute to positive change but also position yourself to thrive in an evolving and socially conscious market. In the upcoming chapters, we'll explore strategies for diverse market conditions and provide insights into the future landscape of the Indian share market. Get ready to embrace a sustainable and purpose-driven investment journey!

Chapter 24: The Holistic Approach to Financial Success

Welcome to the culmination of your journey in

understanding the intricacies of the Indian share market. In this final chapter, we'll explore the

holistic approach to financial success, emphasizing the integration of various elements, from

investment strategies to risk management and psychological resilience.

Integrating Investment Strategies

Balancing Diversification and Concentration
- Explore the delicate balance between diversification and concentration in your portfolio. Understand when to spread investments across various assets and when to focus on high-conviction opportunities.

Strategic Asset Allocation Revisited
- Revisit the concept of strategic asset allocation. Understand how periodically reassessing and adjusting your portfolio's asset mix can align with changing market conditions and your evolving financial goals.

The Psychology of Long-Term Success

Patience as a Virtue
- Reaffirm the virtue of patience in the world of investing. Understand that successful investors exhibit the discipline to withstand short-term market fluctuations while maintaining a focus on long-term objectives.

Emotional Intelligence in Financial Decision-Making
- Explore the role of emotional intelligence in financial decision-making. Understand how self-awareness, self-regulation, motivation, empathy, and social skills contribute to better financial choices.

Advanced Risk Management Strategies

Tailoring Risk Management to Your Portfolio
- Tailor your risk management strategies to your specific portfolio and risk tolerance. Understand that risk is inherent in investing, but strategic risk management can mitigate potential downsides.

Stress Testing for Resilience
- Implement stress testing for your portfolio. Simulate various market scenarios to assess how your investments may perform under adverse conditions, allowing you to make informed adjustments.

The Art of Continuous Learning

Staying Informed in a Dynamic Market
- Embrace the art of continuous learning. Recognize that the financial landscape evolves, and staying informed about market trends, regulations, and technological advancements is crucial for informed decision-making.

Adapting to Technological Innovations
- Stay adaptable to technological innovations. Explore new tools, platforms, and strategies that leverage advancements in financial technology to enhance your investment approach.

Building a Financial Support Network

Engaging with Financial Communities
- Engage with financial communities. Join forums, discussion groups, or investment clubs where you can share experiences, exchange insights, and build a supportive network.

Seeking Professional Guidance When Needed
- Recognize the value of seeking professional guidance. Whether through financial advisors, investment professionals, or mentors, having a trusted support system can provide valuable perspectives.

A Sustainable Approach to Investing

Sustainability in Financial Decision-Making

- Infuse sustainability into your financial decision-making. Consider the long-term impact of your investments on the environment, society, and governance, aligning your portfolio with your values.

Ethical Considerations in Investments

- Assess the ethical considerations of your investments. Understand the business practices of the companies you invest in and ensure alignment with your ethical standards.

Achieving a Work-Life-Financial Balance

Balancing Career and Financial Goals

- Achieve a balance between your career and financial goals. Recognize that financial success is a holistic endeavor, and maintaining a healthy work-life balance contributes to overall well-being.

Leveraging Financial Success for Personal Fulfillment

- Leverage financial success for personal fulfillment. Explore opportunities for philanthropy, pursuing passions, or contributing to causes that align with your values.

The Continuous Journey of Financial Growth

Viewing Financial Success as a Journey

- View financial success as an ongoing journey. Understand that it's not a destination but a continuous process of learning, adapting, and growing.

The Role of Legacy Planning

- Consider legacy planning. Reflect on how you can leave a positive impact on future generations, whether through financial bequests, knowledge transfer, or charitable contributions.

Embracing the Holistic Approach

As we conclude this comprehensive exploration of the Indian share market, embrace the holistic approach to financial success. Recognize that it involves a harmonious integration of investment strategies, risk management, psychological resilience, and a commitment to continuous learning. May your financial journey be fulfilling, resilient, and marked by sustainable success.

Thank you for joining us on this educational journey. Wishing you the best in your endeavors in the Indian share market and beyond.

Chapter 25: Adaptive Strategies for Diverse Market Conditions

Navigating the Dynamic Terrain of the Indian Share Market

In this chapter, we'll delve into adaptive investment strategies designed to thrive in diverse market conditions. As markets evolve, understanding how to adjust your approach is essential for maximizing returns and mitigating risks.

Bull Markets: Capitalizing on Optimism

Riding the Momentum
- Explore strategies for capitalizing on bullish markets. During periods of optimism, investors can focus on momentum investing, riding the upward trends of high-performing stocks.

Sector Rotation
- Understand the concept of sector rotation in bull markets. As economic conditions shift, certain sectors may outperform others, providing opportunities for strategic reallocation.

Bear Markets: Preserving Capital in Downturns

Defensive Strategies
- Dive into defensive strategies for bear markets. During downturns, focus on defensive sectors and assets that traditionally exhibit resilience, such as utilities and dividend-paying stocks.

Risk Hedging Techniques
- Explore risk-hedging techniques to protect your portfolio in bearish conditions. Options, inverse ETFs, and other hedging instruments can act as safeguards against significant market declines.

Sideways Markets: Capitalizing on Range-Bound Movements

Options Trading Strategies
- Discover options trading strategies suitable for sideways markets. Options can be leveraged to generate income, especially when underlying securities are trading within a range.

Tactical Asset Allocation
- Implement tactical asset allocation in periods of market stagnation. By adjusting the allocation of assets based on prevailing conditions, investors can optimize returns during sideways movements.

Volatile Markets: Seizing Opportunities Amid Turbulence

Contrarian Investing
- Embrace contrarian investing during volatile periods. Contrarians go against prevailing market sentiment, identifying opportunities in stocks that may be undervalued due to short-term challenges.

Dynamic Sector Rotation
- Engage in dynamic sector rotation to adapt to changing market dynamics. During volatility, sectors may experience rapid shifts in performance, presenting opportunities for strategic adjustments.

Trend Following in Dynamic Environments

Utilizing Trend Following Strategies
- Understand the principles of trend following. In dynamic environments, trend-following strategies involve identifying and riding market trends, whether upward or downward, to optimize returns.

Technical Analysis for Market Timing
- Leverage technical analysis for market timing. Analyzing price charts, trends, and indicators can provide valuable insights for making informed decisions in response to evolving market conditions.

Long-Term Investing: The Power of Patience

Compounding Wealth Over Time
- Revisit the principles of long-term investing. While adapting to short-term conditions is crucial, maintaining a focus on compounding wealth over time through a disciplined long-term strategy remains a cornerstone.

Rebalancing for Long-Term Success
- Emphasize the importance of periodic rebalancing for long-term success. Adjust your portfolio to maintain alignment with your risk tolerance and financial goals, ensuring a resilient approach over the years.

The Art of Adaptability

As we conclude this chapter, remember that adaptability is the hallmark of successful investing. By understanding the nuances of diverse market conditions and employing strategies tailored to each environment, you empower yourself to navigate the dynamic terrain of the Indian share market. In the forthcoming chapters, we'll explore cutting-edge technologies and their impact on the future of investing, ensuring you stay at the forefront of the financial landscape. Get ready to embrace the art of adaptability in your investment journey!

Chapter 26: Fintech Revolution - Transforming the Investment Landscape

Embracing Technological Advancements for Financial Success

In this chapter, we'll explore the Fintech revolution, a transformative wave of technological innovations that is reshaping the investment landscape. Understanding and harnessing these advancements is essential for investors looking to stay competitive in the fast-paced world of finance.

Robo-Advisors and Algorithmic Investing

Automated Portfolio Management
- Delve into the world of Robo-Advisors. These digital platforms utilize algorithms to create and manage diversified investment portfolios, catering to individual risk profiles and financial goals.

Algorithmic Trading Strategies
- Explore advanced algorithmic trading strategies. Algorithms can analyze market data, execute trades, and adapt to changing conditions at speeds unattainable through traditional manual trading.

Peer-to-Peer Lending and Crowdfunding

Direct Lending Platforms
- Explore the concept of peer-to-peer lending. Investors can lend directly to individuals or small businesses through online platforms, earning returns based on interest rates.

Equity Crowdfunding
- Understand the rise of equity crowdfunding. Investors can participate in funding startups and small businesses, gaining equity stakes in exchange for financial support.

Cryptocurrencies and Decentralized Finance (DeFi)

Digital Asset Investments
- Explore the world of cryptocurrencies as digital assets. Cryptocurrencies like Bitcoin and Ethereum offer alternative investment opportunities with unique risk and return profiles.

Decentralized Finance Platforms
- Understand the concept of Decentralized Finance (DeFi). These platforms leverage blockchain technology to provide financial services without traditional intermediaries, opening new avenues for investors.

Mobile Trading Apps and Accessibility

On-the-Go Trading
- Embrace the convenience of mobile trading apps. Investors can access real-time market data, execute trades, and manage portfolios from their mobile devices, enhancing flexibility and responsiveness.

Financial Inclusion Through Apps
- Explore how Fintech apps contribute to financial inclusion. These apps often cater to underserved populations, providing access to banking, investment, and payment services.

Big Data Analytics for Market Insights

Data-Driven Decision-Making

- Understand the role of Big Data analytics in financial markets. Fintech firms leverage vast datasets to gain insights into market trends, customer behavior, and investment opportunities.

Personalized Financial Recommendations

- Explore how Fintech utilizes data for personalized financial recommendations. Machine learning algorithms analyze individual financial patterns to offer tailored advice and product recommendations.

Cybersecurity in Fintech

Ensuring Financial Security

- Recognize the importance of cybersecurity in the Fintech landscape. As digital transactions become prevalent, ensuring the security of financial data and transactions is paramount.

Blockchain for Secure Transactions

- Explore how blockchain technology enhances security in Fintech. The decentralized and immutable nature of blockchain provides a secure foundation for financial transactions.

Continuous Learning in the Fintech Era

Staying Informed about Innovations

- Embrace a mindset of continuous learning in the Fintech era. Stay informed about emerging technologies, regulations, and innovations to make informed decisions in the evolving financial landscape.

Practical Application Through Simulations

- Engage in practical simulations to familiarize yourself with Fintech tools and platforms. Simulations offer hands-on experience, allowing you to navigate the digital landscape with confidence.

Future-Forward Investment

As we conclude this chapter, remember that the Fintech revolution opens new horizons for investors. By embracing technological advancements, you position yourself to leverage innovative tools and platforms, enhancing your capabilities in the ever-evolving financial landscape. In the upcoming chapters, we'll explore strategies for effective risk management and delve into the psychology of successful investing. Get ready to shape your investment future with the power of Fintech!

Chapter 27: The Psychology of Successful Investing

Mastering the Mindset for Financial Triumph

In this chapter, we'll delve into the psychology of successful investing, unraveling the intricate web of emotions, biases, and decision-making processes that significantly influence investment outcomes. Understanding and mastering this psychological aspect is paramount for achieving lasting success in the world of finance.

Emotional Intelligence in Investing

Embracing Emotional Awareness
- Explore the importance of emotional awareness in investing. Recognizing and understanding your own emotions is crucial for making rational and well-informed investment decisions.

Managing Emotional Responses to Market Volatility
- Develop strategies for managing emotional responses during market volatility. Learn how to stay composed, avoid impulsive actions, and make decisions based on a rational assessment of market conditions.

Behavioral Biases and Their Impact

Overcoming Confirmation Bias
- Understand the impact of confirmation bias in investment decisions. Explore techniques to overcome the tendency to seek information that confirms preexisting beliefs, promoting a more objective analysis.

Avoiding Herd Mentality
- Delve into the dangers of herd mentality in investing. Learn how to resist the pressure to follow the crowd and make independent decisions based on thorough research and analysis.

Patience and Discipline

The Virtue of Patience
- Embrace the virtue of patience in investing. Recognize that successful investing is a long-term endeavor, and avoid succumbing to the impatience that can lead to hasty and regrettable decisions.

Discipline in Adhering to a Strategy
- Establish and adhere to a disciplined investment strategy. Whether it's value investing, growth investing, or a balanced approach, discipline ensures consistency and helps weather market fluctuations.

Goal-Oriented Investing

Setting Clear and Achievable Goals
- Define clear and achievable investment goals. Having a well-defined roadmap provides a sense of purpose and direction, guiding your investment decisions toward fulfilling your financial aspirations.

Aligning Investments with Life Goals
- Align investments with broader life goals. Consider how your financial decisions contribute to long-term objectives such as homeownership, education, or retirement, fostering a holistic approach to investing.

Learning from Mistakes and Setbacks

Embracing Mistakes as Learning Opportunities
- View mistakes as valuable learning opportunities. Analyze investment decisions that didn't go as planned, identify areas for improvement, and use these lessons to enhance future strategies.

Resilience in the Face of Setbacks
- Develop resilience to navigate setbacks. Financial markets are inherently unpredictable, and setbacks are inevitable. Resilience enables you to bounce back, learn, and continue on your investment journey.

Continuous Learning and Adaptability

Staying Informed About Market Developments
- Embrace continuous learning about market developments. Stay informed about economic trends, industry shifts, and geopolitical events, empowering you to make well-informed decisions.

Adapting to Changing Market Conditions
- Cultivate adaptability in response to changing market conditions. Recognize that flexibility is a key attribute of successful investors who can adjust their strategies based on evolving circumstances.

Professional Guidance and Mentorship

Seeking Advice from Financial Experts
- Consider seeking advice from financial experts. Engaging with professional advisors provides insights, guidance, and a structured approach to navigating complex financial landscapes.

Mentorship for Personal Growth
- Explore the benefits of mentorship in personal growth. Learning from experienced investors can provide valuable perspectives, practical insights, and a support system for your investment journey.

The Psychology of Wealth Accumulation

As we conclude this chapter, remember that mastering the psychology of successful investing is an ongoing journey. By cultivating emotional intelligence, overcoming biases, embracing patience, and learning from experiences, you lay the foundation for a resilient and successful investment mindset. In the upcoming chapters, we'll explore advanced portfolio management strategies and delve into sustainable investing practices. Get ready to elevate your investment psychology and achieve financial triumph!

Chapter 28: Advanced Portfolio Management Strategies

Optimizing Your Investments for Peak Performance

In this chapter, we'll delve into advanced portfolio management strategies, designed to optimize your investments for peak performance. As you progress in your investment journey, understanding these strategies becomes pivotal for achieving enhanced returns and mitigating risks.

Tactical Asset Allocation

Strategic Rebalancing Techniques
- Explore strategic rebalancing techniques in tactical asset allocation. Adjusting portfolio weights based on prevailing market conditions allows you to capitalize on opportunities and maintain an optimal risk-return profile.

Dynamic Asset Allocation Models
- Dive into dynamic asset allocation models. These models adapt to changing economic environments, adjusting the allocation of assets to align with evolving market dynamics.

Factor-Based Investing

Understanding Factor Investing
- Explore factor investing strategies. Factors such as value, size, momentum, and quality can be leveraged to construct portfolios that target specific risk and return characteristics.

Multi-Factor Investing Approaches
- Delve into multi-factor investing approaches. Combining multiple factors allows for a more diversified and robust portfolio that can outperform traditional market-cap-weighted strategies.

Alternative Investments

Diversifying with Alternatives
- Consider the role of alternative investments in diversification. Assets such as real estate, commodities, and private equity can provide additional sources of return and reduce overall portfolio risk.

Hedging with Options and Derivatives
- Explore the use of options and derivatives for hedging purposes. These instruments can act as risk management tools, offering protection against adverse market movements.

Quantitative Investing

Utilizing Quantitative Models
- Understand the application of quantitative models in investing. These models use mathematical and statistical techniques to analyze data and identify investment opportunities.

Algorithmic Trading Strategies
- Explore algorithmic trading strategies within quantitative investing. Algorithmic models can execute trades at optimal prices and frequencies, enhancing portfolio efficiency.

Portfolio Optimization Techniques

Modern Portfolio Theory (MPT)
- Revisit Modern Portfolio Theory (MPT). MPT emphasizes diversification to achieve optimal risk-adjusted returns and forms the foundation for constructing well-balanced portfolios.

Post-Modern Portfolio Theory (PMPT)
- Delve into Post-Modern Portfolio Theory (PMPT). PMPT extends MPT by considering additional factors such as market dynamics and investor behavior to enhance portfolio construction.

Risk Parity Strategies

Balancing Risk Across Assets
- Explore risk parity strategies. These approaches allocate risk equally across different assets, aiming to achieve a more balanced and stable portfolio.

Risk-Parity-Managed Funds
- Understand the concept of risk-parity-managed funds. These funds dynamically adjust asset allocations based on volatility, seeking to maintain consistent risk exposure.

Sustainable and ESG Investing Integration

ESG Considerations in Portfolio Construction
- Integrate Environmental, Social, and Governance (ESG) considerations into portfolio construction. ESG factors can be used as additional criteria for selecting investments aligned with ethical and sustainable principles.

Sustainable Investing Performance Metrics
- Explore sustainable investing performance metrics. Assessing the financial performance of companies alongside their ESG practices provides a comprehensive evaluation for sustainable portfolios.

Factor Rotation Strategies

Adapting to Factor Cycles
- Explore factor rotation strategies. These strategies involve adjusting factor exposures based on market conditions and the prevailing stage of the economic cycle.

Factor Timing Models
- Understand factor timing models. These models aim to identify opportune times to overweight or underweight specific factors, enhancing the potential for outperformance.

The Art and Science of Portfolio Management

As we conclude this chapter, remember that advanced portfolio management involves both art and science. By incorporating these strategies into your investment approach, you elevate your ability to navigate complex markets, adapt to changing conditions, and optimize your portfolio for sustained success. In the upcoming chapters, we'll explore the impact of technology on investment strategies and delve into the ever-evolving landscape of sustainable investing. Get ready to further refine your portfolio management skills!

Chapter 29: Sustainable Investing - Beyond Financial Returns

Navigating the Path to a Sustainable Future

In this chapter, we'll further explore the realm of sustainable investing, delving deeper into its various facets and uncovering the profound impact it can have beyond financial returns. As global awareness grows, understanding the intricacies of sustainable investing becomes crucial for investors aiming to make a positive difference in the world.

Green Bonds and Impact Investments

Supporting Environmental Initiatives
- Explore the world of green bonds. These fixed-income instruments are specifically designated to fund projects with environmental benefits, allowing investors to support sustainability initiatives.

Measuring Impact in Impact Investments
- Understand impact investments and how they measure positive contributions to social and environmental causes. Impact investing goes beyond financial returns, aiming to create meaningful and measurable change.

Community Development Investments

Investing in Local Communities
- Delve into community development investments. By directing capital towards projects that uplift local communities, investors can play a role in fostering economic growth and social well-being.

Affordable Housing Initiatives
- Explore sustainable investments in affordable housing. Supporting projects that address housing challenges contributes to both social impact and the creation of sustainable, resilient communities.

Ethical Supply Chain Investments

Promoting Ethical Business Practices
- Investigate the concept of ethical supply chain investments. By supporting companies with transparent and ethical supply chain practices, investors can encourage responsible corporate behavior.

Addressing Social and Labor Issues
- Understand how investments can address social and labor issues within supply chains. Investors can influence positive change by aligning with companies committed to fair labor practices and social responsibility.

Regenerative Agriculture Investments

Sustainable Farming Practices
- Explore regenerative agriculture investments. By supporting sustainable and environmentally friendly farming practices, investors contribute to soil health, biodiversity, and the overall resilience of the agricultural sector.

Impacts on Climate Change Mitigation
- Understand the role of regenerative agriculture in climate change mitigation. Investments in sustainable farming practices can help sequester carbon, reduce greenhouse gas emissions, and promote climate resilience.

Socially Responsible Investing (SRI)

Aligning Investments with Values
- Revisit socially responsible investing (SRI) principles. SRI allows investors to align their portfolios with personal values, avoiding investments in companies that contradict ethical or moral beliefs.

Screening for Responsible Practices
- Explore screening methods in socially responsible investing. Investors can screen out companies involved in activities deemed harmful or unethical while favoring those with positive social and environmental practices.

Gender-Lens Investing

Promoting Gender Equality
- Delve into gender-lens investing. This approach directs capital towards companies that actively promote gender equality, fostering diversity and inclusion within corporate structures.

Investing in Women-Led Enterprises
- Understand the impact of investing in women-led enterprises. Supporting women entrepreneurs and businesses contributes to economic empowerment and the overall advancement of gender equality.

Impact Measurement and Reporting

Metrics for Social and Environmental Impact
- Explore metrics used for measuring social and environmental impact. Robust impact measurement and reporting allow investors to assess the tangible effects of their sustainable investments.

Transparency in Impact Reporting
- Recognize the importance of transparency in impact reporting. Investors can make more informed decisions when companies provide clear and comprehensive reports on their sustainability efforts.

Sustainable Investing as a Long-Term Strategy

Aligning with Future Trends
- Understand how sustainable investing aligns with future trends. As global awareness of environmental and social issues increases, sustainable investments are poised to become integral to long-term investment strategies.

Resilience in the Face of Global Challenges
- Explore how sustainable investments contribute to portfolio resilience. Companies with strong ESG practices are often better equipped to navigate global challenges, providing stability in unpredictable environments.

Embracing a Sustainable Investment Journey

As we conclude this chapter, remember that sustainable investing transcends financial gains, offering a pathway to positive change. By navigating various sustainable investment avenues, you not only contribute to global well-being but also position yourself for long-term success in an evolving and socially conscious market. In the upcoming chapters, we'll delve into risk management strategies and explore the psychological aspects of successful investing. Get ready to further refine your investment approach for a sustainable and prosperous future!

Chapter 30: Mastering Risk Management in Investment Strategies

Navigating the Sea of Uncertainty with Confidence

In this chapter, we will explore the critical aspect of risk management in investment strategies. Mastering risk is essential for preserving capital, achieving consistent returns, and navigating the uncertainties inherent in financial markets. Let's delve into strategies that empower investors to manage risk effectively.

Diversification Strategies

Building a Robust Portfolio
- Explore the art of diversification. Building a well-diversified portfolio across different asset classes, industries, and geographies helps mitigate risks associated with individual investments.

Correlation Analysis for Optimal Allocation

- Understand correlation analysis. Identifying assets with low correlations can enhance the effectiveness of diversification, providing a more balanced and resilient portfolio.

Risk-Adjusted Return Metrics

Sharpe Ratio and Beyond
- Dive into risk-adjusted return metrics. The Sharpe ratio, Sortino ratio, and other measures help investors assess returns in relation to the level of risk taken, aiding in the evaluation of investment performance.

Volatility as a Risk Indicator
- Explore the role of volatility as a risk indicator. Volatility measures provide insights into the potential price fluctuations of an investment, helping investors gauge and manage risk exposure.

Tail Risk Hedging Strategies

Utilizing Options for Tail Risk Protection
- Understand how options can be used for tail risk hedging. Options strategies, such as buying protective puts, provide insurance against extreme market downturns.

Risk Mitigation Through Diversifying Strategies
- Explore diversifying strategies for tail risk mitigation. Investments with low correlation to traditional assets, such as managed futures and alternative investments, can act as buffers during severe market events.

Stress Testing Portfolios

Assessing Portfolio Resilience
- Learn the importance of stress testing portfolios. Stress tests simulate adverse market conditions, helping investors assess how their portfolios may perform during periods of extreme volatility.

Scenario Analysis for Contingency Planning
- Incorporate scenario analysis into risk management. Evaluating different market scenarios allows investors to develop contingency plans and make informed decisions based on potential outcomes.

Risk Parity and Equal Weighting

Balancing Risk Across Assets
- Revisit risk parity strategies. These approaches allocate risk equally among different assets, providing a balanced risk exposure that can enhance portfolio stability.

Equal Weighting for Diversification

- Explore the concept of equal weighting in portfolio construction. Assigning equal weight to each holding can prevent concentration risk and enhance diversification.

Systematic and Unsystematic Risk

Understanding Systematic Risk Factors
- Distinguish between systematic and unsystematic risk. Systematic risks are market-wide factors that impact all investments, while unsystematic risks are specific to individual assets.

Effective Use of Risk Models
- Utilize risk models to identify and manage systematic and unsystematic risks. Sophisticated risk models help investors quantify and mitigate potential threats to their portfolios.

Active Risk Management Strategies

Continuous Monitoring of Portfolio Positions
- Embrace continuous monitoring of portfolio positions. Regularly reassessing the risk exposure of individual holdings allows for prompt adjustments in response to changing market conditions.

Dynamic Asset Allocation for Risk Control
- Implement dynamic asset allocation strategies for risk control. Adapting asset weights based on prevailing market conditions helps investors maintain a risk profile aligned with their investment objectives.

Behavioral Aspects of Risk Management

Emotional Resilience During Market Volatility
- Understand the behavioral aspects of risk management. Emotional resilience during market volatility is crucial for avoiding impulsive decisions that may compromise long-term financial goals.

Discipline in Adhering to Risk Mitigation Strategies
- Cultivate discipline in adhering to risk mitigation strategies. A disciplined approach ensures that risk management measures are consistently applied, even in challenging market environments.

Holistic Approach to Risk Management

Integration of Risk in Investment Process
- Integrate risk management into the entire investment process. Adopting a holistic approach ensures that risk considerations are fundamental to decision-making at every stage.

Educating Stakeholders on Risk

- Educate stakeholders on risk management strategies. Transparent communication about risk factors and mitigation measures fosters understanding and confidence among investors.

Building a Resilient Investment Future

As we conclude this chapter, remember that mastering risk management is an ongoing journey that requires diligence and adaptability. By incorporating these strategies into your investment approach, you empower yourself to navigate the complexities of financial markets with confidence. In the upcoming chapters, we'll explore the psychology of successful investing and delve into the impact of technology on investment strategies. Get ready to further refine your skills for a resilient and prosperous investment future!

Chapter 31: The Impact of Technology on Modern Investing

Navigating the Digital Frontier for Enhanced Returns

In this chapter, we'll explore the profound impact of technology on modern investing. The integration of cutting-edge tools, data analytics, and digital platforms has transformed the investment landscape. Understanding and harnessing these technological advancements is crucial for investors looking to stay ahead in a rapidly evolving market.

Robo-Advisors and Algorithmic Trading

Efficiency Through Automation
- Explore the rise of Robo-Advisors. These automated platforms use algorithms to create and manage investment portfolios, providing cost-effective and efficient solutions for investors.

Algorithmic Trading for Precision
- Dive into the world of algorithmic trading. Algorithms analyze market data at speeds unattainable by humans, executing trades with precision and adapting to changing market conditions.

Artificial Intelligence in Investment Decision-Making

Data-Driven Investment Insights
- Understand the role of artificial intelligence (AI) in investment decision-making. AI algorithms analyze vast datasets to identify patterns, trends, and potential investment opportunities.

Predictive Analytics for Market Trends
- Explore predictive analytics in forecasting market trends. AI-driven models can offer insights into future price movements, helping investors make informed decisions.

Blockchain and Cryptocurrencies

Decentralized Transactions with Blockchain
- Delve into the impact of blockchain on financial transactions. Blockchain technology, through its decentralized and secure nature, has influenced the development of cryptocurrencies and transformed the way assets are transferred.

Cryptocurrencies as Alternative Investments
- Explore the role of cryptocurrencies as alternative investments. Digital assets like Bitcoin and Ethereum have gained popularity as investors seek diversification in a rapidly changing financial landscape.

Big Data Analytics for Market Intelligence

Informed Decision-Making with Big Data
- Understand how Big Data analytics provide market intelligence. Analyzing large datasets helps investors gain insights into market trends, customer behavior, and potential risks.

Personalized Investment Strategies
- Explore the use of Big Data for personalized investment strategies. Tailoring investment approaches based on individual preferences and financial goals enhances the overall investor experience.

Mobile Trading Apps and Accessibility

On-the-Go Investing
- Embrace the convenience of mobile trading apps. Investors can monitor markets, execute trades, and manage portfolios from anywhere, enhancing accessibility and responsiveness.

Financial Inclusion Through Mobile Apps
- Explore how mobile apps contribute to financial inclusion. These apps often cater to underserved populations, providing access to banking, investment, and payment services through mobile devices.

Machine Learning in Risk Management

Proactive Risk Identification
- Utilize machine learning for proactive risk identification. Advanced algorithms can assess potential risks in real-time, allowing investors to implement risk management strategies more effectively.

Dynamic Portfolio Adjustments
- Explore how machine learning enables dynamic portfolio adjustments. Algorithms can adapt portfolios based on changing market conditions, optimizing risk-return profiles.

Cybersecurity in the Digital Era

Ensuring Financial Security
- Recognize the importance of cybersecurity in the digital era. As financial transactions move online, robust cybersecurity measures are essential to safeguard sensitive financial information.

Blockchain for Enhanced Security
- Explore how blockchain enhances security in financial transactions. The decentralized and immutable nature of blockchain provides a secure foundation for digital asset transfers.

Continuous Learning and Adaptation

Staying Informed About Technological Advances
- Embrace continuous learning about technological advances. Staying informed about emerging technologies, such as AI, blockchain, and machine learning, positions investors to adapt to the evolving digital landscape.

Practical Application Through Simulations
- Engage in practical simulations to familiarize yourself with technological tools. Simulations offer hands-on experience, allowing investors to navigate digital platforms and technologies with confidence.

Future-Forward Investing

As we conclude this chapter, remember that embracing technology is integral to future-forward investing. By harnessing the power of digital tools, data analytics, and emerging technologies, investors can gain a competitive edge in a rapidly evolving market. In the upcoming chapters, we'll explore advanced portfolio management strategies and delve into sustainable investing practices. Get ready to further refine your investment approach in the digital era!

Chapter 32: Exploring Sustainable Practices in Modern Investing

Aligning Portfolios with Environmental, Social, and Governance (ESG) Values

In this chapter, we'll explore the growing importance of sustainable investing practices in the modern investment landscape. Investors are increasingly recognizing the impact of their financial decisions on the world. Understanding and incorporating ESG principles can not only contribute to positive change but also enhance the long-term resilience of investment portfolios.

Environmental Considerations in Investments

Renewable Energy Investments
- Explore the role of investments in renewable energy. Supporting projects such as solar and wind energy not only aligns with environmental sustainability but also taps into the potential of a rapidly expanding industry.

Climate Change Resilience in Portfolios
- Understand the importance of climate change resilience in portfolios. Investing in companies with robust environmental practices can mitigate risks associated with climate-related events and regulatory changes.

Socially Responsible Investment (SRI) Strategies

Promoting Diversity and Inclusion
- Delve into socially responsible investment strategies. Investing in companies that prioritize diversity and inclusion contributes to social progress and fosters a corporate culture of equality.

Ethical Supply Chain Investments
- Explore ethical supply chain investments. Supporting companies with transparent and ethical supply chain practices promotes responsible business conduct and contributes to positive social impact.

Governance and Ethical Corporate Practices

Emphasizing Strong Corporate Governance
- Understand the significance of strong corporate governance. Companies with transparent governance structures and ethical practices are often better positioned for long-term success and investor confidence.

Avoiding Investments with Governance Risks
- Explore the identification and avoidance of investments with governance risks. Understanding the governance structures of companies helps investors make informed decisions that align with their values.

Impact Measurement and Reporting

Quantifying Social and Environmental Impact
- Explore metrics for quantifying social and environmental impact. Investors can use transparent reporting and measurable metrics to assess the tangible effects of their sustainable investments.

Integration of Impact Reporting in Decision-Making
- Recognize the integration of impact reporting in decision-making. Investors can make more informed choices when companies provide clear and comprehensive reports on their ESG practices and their overall impact.

Sustainable Development Goals (SDGs) and Investments

Investing in Solutions for Global Challenges

- Understand how investments can contribute to Sustainable Development Goals (SDGs). Aligning investment strategies with global challenges, such as poverty alleviation and clean water access, supports broader societal objectives.

Measuring Contributions to SDGs

- Explore methodologies for measuring contributions to SDGs. Investors can use frameworks and indicators to assess how their investments align with specific sustainable development targets.

ESG Integration in Investment Decisions

Incorporating ESG Factors in Analysis

- Embrace the integration of ESG factors in investment analysis. Considering environmental, social, and governance criteria alongside traditional financial metrics provides a more comprehensive view of potential investments.

Building ESG-Focused Portfolios

- Explore the construction of ESG-focused portfolios. Building a portfolio that prioritizes companies with strong ESG practices allows investors to align their financial goals with sustainable values.

Sustainable Investing as a Long-Term Strategy

Aligning with Evolving Investor Values

- Understand how sustainable investing aligns with evolving investor values. As awareness grows, incorporating ESG considerations becomes integral to long-term investment strategies.

Enhancing Portfolio Resilience

- Explore how sustainable investments contribute to portfolio resilience. Companies with robust ESG practices are often better equipped to navigate challenges, providing stability in unpredictable market environments.

Nurturing a Sustainable Investment Journey

As we conclude this chapter, remember that sustainable investing is not just a trend but a transformative approach to wealth creation. By aligning portfolios with ESG values, investors can contribute to positive change while potentially enjoying financial success. In the upcoming chapters, we'll delve into risk management strategies and explore the psychological aspects of successful investing. Get ready to further refine your investment approach for a resilient and prosperous future!

Chapter 33: Unveiling the Top 30 Questions in Indian Share Market

A Comprehensive Guide to Addressing Investor Queries

In this chapter, we'll delve into the top 30 questions that most people ask about the Indian share market. Whether you're a seasoned investor or a newcomer, understanding the intricacies of the market is crucial. Let's unravel common queries and provide comprehensive answers to empower investors with the knowledge they need for informed decision-making.

Market Fundamentals

What is the BSE and NSE, and how do they differ?

- Explore the Bombay Stock Exchange (BSE) and the National Stock Exchange (NSE) and understand the key differences in their operations and indices.

How does the Indian share market function?

- Gain insights into the functioning of the Indian share market, including the role of stock exchanges, regulators, and market participants.

What are indices, and how are they used in the stock market?

- Understand stock market indices and their significance in measuring the performance of the overall market or specific sectors.

Stock Selection and Analysis

How do I choose stocks for investment?

- Explore fundamental and technical analysis methods to assist in selecting stocks based on financial health, market trends, and other relevant factors.

What is the significance of P/E ratio and how is it calculated?

- Understand the Price-to-Earnings (P/E) ratio, a key valuation metric, and learn how to calculate it for evaluating stock attractiveness.

How do dividends work, and why are they important for investors?

- Delve into the concept of dividends, their impact on shareholder returns, and how companies distribute profits to investors.

Risk Management and Strategies

What are the risk factors associated with stock market investments?

- Explore various risks, including market risk, liquidity risk, and systemic risk, to make informed decisions on risk management.

How can I create a diversified investment portfolio?

- Learn the principles of diversification and portfolio construction to spread risk and optimize returns.

What is systematic investment planning (SIP), and how does it work?

- Understand the concept of SIP, a disciplined approach to investing in mutual funds, and its benefits for long-term wealth creation.

Market Trends and Timing

How can I identify market trends and potential investment opportunities?

- Explore tools and techniques for recognizing market trends and identifying investment opportunities in various market conditions.

Is market timing essential for successful investing?

- Understand the challenges and considerations associated with market timing and the importance of a long-term investment approach.

What are bull and bear markets, and how do they impact investments?

- Explore the characteristics of bull and bear markets and strategies to navigate each phase effectively.

Investment Strategies

How can I align investments with financial goals and risk tolerance?
- Learn the importance of aligning investments with specific financial goals and tailoring strategies based on risk tolerance.

What are blue-chip stocks, and why are they considered stable investments?
- Understand the characteristics of blue-chip stocks and their reputation for stability and consistent performance.

How can I invest in mutual funds, and what are the types available?
- Explore the process of investing in mutual funds and the various types of funds catering to different investor preferences.

Market Regulations and Ethics

What role do regulatory bodies play in the Indian share market?
- Gain insights into the regulatory framework of the Indian share market, including the Securities and Exchange Board of India (SEBI).

How can I avoid fraud and unethical practices in the stock market?
- Learn about common fraudulent practices and ethical considerations to safeguard investments and maintain market integrity.

What are insider trading and its consequences?
- Understand the concept of insider trading and the legal consequences associated with trading based on non-public information.

Trading and Execution

How do I place buy and sell orders in the stock market?
- Get familiar with the process of placing orders, including market orders, limit orders, and stop-loss orders.

What is the significance of trading volumes in the stock market?
- Understand the importance of trading volumes in assessing market liquidity and potential price movements.

How can I use technical analysis for better trading decisions?
- Explore key technical analysis tools and indicators to enhance trading decisions and identify entry and exit points.

Financial Literacy and Education

Where can I find reliable financial information and resources?

- Discover reputable sources for financial information, market updates, and educational resources to stay informed.

How can I enhance my financial literacy for better investment decisions?

- Learn practical steps to improve financial literacy, including reading financial reports, attending workshops, and staying updated on market trends.

What role do financial advisors play, and how do I choose one?

- Understand the role of financial advisors, the types of advice they provide, and criteria for selecting a trustworthy advisor.

Market Volatility and Corrections

How should I navigate market volatility and corrections?

- Develop strategies to navigate market volatility and corrections, including maintaining a long-term perspective and reviewing investment portfolios.

What are circuit breakers, and how do they impact trading during extreme volatility?

- Explore the concept of circuit breakers and their role in temporarily halting trading during significant market movements.

Taxation and Investment Returns

How are stock market gains taxed in India?

- Understand the taxation of capital gains and dividends from stock market investments to optimize tax liabilities.

What are the implications of dividend distribution tax (DDT) on investors?

- Explore the impact of dividend distribution tax and its implications for investors receiving dividends from companies.

Future of the Indian Share Market

What trends and innovations can we expect in the future of the Indian share market?

- Anticipate future trends, technological advancements, and regulatory changes shaping the landscape of the Indian share market.

How can I stay resilient as an investor amid market uncertainties?

- Develop a resilient mindset and strategies to navigate uncertainties, market fluctuations, and external factors that may impact investments.

In this chapter, we'll address the next top 30 questions that most investors, both beginners and seasoned ones, often have when navigating the complexities of the Indian share market. These questions cover a wide range of topics, providing clarity and guidance for making informed investment decisions.

**How do I get started in the Indian share market as a beginner?
What are the key factors to consider before selecting a stock to invest in?
How does market sentiment impact stock prices, and how can I navigate it?
What are the risks associated with investing in the Indian share market?
How do I create a well-diversified portfolio?
What role does research play in successful stock selection?
Can you explain the impact of economic indicators on the stock market?
How do I analyze a company's financial statements before investing?
What are the different types of investment strategies, and which one suits me?
How can I manage risks effectively in my portfolio?
What is the significance of dividends, and how do they impact stock prices?
How can I stay updated on market trends and news that affect my investments?
What are the common mistakes to avoid as an investor in the stock market?
How does inflation affect my investment returns, and how can I hedge against it?
Can you explain the concept of market cycles, and how should I navigate them?
How do global events and geopolitical factors impact the Indian share market?
What are the tax implications of stock market investments in India?
How do I interpret technical analysis charts to make better investment decisions?
Can you guide me on choosing between mutual funds and individual stocks?
How does the Foreign Direct Investment (FDI) policy influence stock markets?
What is the role of the Securities and Exchange Board of India (SEBI) in market regulation?
How can I evaluate the management quality of a company before investing?
Are there specific sectors or industries that are currently promising for investment?
What impact does interest rate movement have on stock prices?
How can I develop a disciplined approach to long-term investing?
Is it advisable to time the market, and how can I do it effectively?
What are the implications of corporate actions like stock splits and mergers?
How can I protect my investments during periods of market volatility?
What resources and tools are available for investors to enhance their knowledge?
How can I plan for my financial goals using investments in the stock market?

These questions and answers provide a comprehensive guide to address various aspects of investing in the Indian share market. Whether you're a novice or an experienced investor, having a clear understanding of these topics can contribute to making well-informed and strategic investment decisions.

Empowering Investors for Success

As we conclude this chapter, remember that knowledge is a powerful tool in the world of investing. By addressing these top 60 questions, we aim to empower investors with the information they need to make sound decisions, navigate challenges, and build a successful investment journey. In the upcoming chapters, we'll continue to explore advanced investment strategies and psychological aspects to further refine your skills. Get ready for a comprehensive guide to mastering the art and science of investing in the Indian share market!

Chapter 34: Your Financial Future Starts Now

In this final chapter, let's embark on a journey of self-reflection and proactive planning for a secure

financial future. By combining the knowledge gained from the previous chapters with a

forward-looking mindset, you can set the stage for a successful and fulfilling financial journey.

Crafting Your Financial Vision

Defining Your Financial Goals
- Clearly define your short-term and long-term financial goals. Whether it's buying a home, funding education, or retiring comfortably, having specific objectives provides direction to your financial planning.

Aligning Your Investments with Values
- Consider aligning your investments with your personal values. If sustainability and ethical considerations are important to you, explore investment opportunities that reflect these principles.

Tailoring Your Investment Strategy

Reviewing and Adjusting Your Portfolio
- Regularly review your investment portfolio and make adjustments based on changing market conditions, economic trends, and your evolving financial goals.

Leveraging Tax-Efficient Strategies
- Explore tax-efficient investment strategies to optimize your returns. Utilize tax-saving investment options and stay informed about changes in tax regulations.

Embracing a Growth Mindset

Continuing Your Financial Education
- Embrace a growth mindset by committing to continuous learning. Stay updated on market trends, explore new investment strategies, and seek knowledge that enhances your financial acumen.

Building Resilience in Financial Decision-Making
- Cultivate resilience in financial decision-making. Understand that setbacks are a part of the investment journey, and the ability to adapt and learn from challenges contributes to long-term success.

Seeking Professional Guidance

Engaging with Financial Advisors
- Consider seeking professional guidance from financial advisors. A qualified advisor can provide personalized insights, help refine your financial goals, and offer strategies to achieve them.

Periodic Financial Check-ins
- Schedule periodic financial check-ins to assess your progress towards your goals. Use these check-ins to make informed adjustments to your investment and financial planning strategies.

Fostering Financial Wellness

Balancing Lifestyle and Financial Aspirations
- Strike a balance between your desired lifestyle and financial aspirations. Avoid overspending, focus on savings, and make intentional choices that align with your financial goals.

Emergency Fund Preparedness
- Prioritize the creation of an emergency fund. Having a financial safety net ensures that unexpected expenses do not derail your long-term investment plans.

Leaving a Financial Legacy

Legacy Planning and Estate Management
- Consider legacy planning and estate management. Determine how you want your assets to be distributed and the impact you wish to leave on future generations.

Sharing Financial Knowledge
- Share your financial knowledge with friends and family. Empowering others with financial literacy contributes to a culture of informed decision-making.

The Ongoing Journey

As we conclude this comprehensive guide to navigating the Indian share market and crafting a secure financial future, remember that your journey is ongoing. Adaptability, continuous learning, and a strategic mindset are the keys to financial success. May your path be marked by informed decisions, resilience, and the achievement of your financial aspirations. Happy investing!

Conclusion

The "Bulls, Bears, and Beyond of Indian Share Market" ebook is your comprehensive guide to not only understanding the nuances of the market but also mastering the art of investing. As you navigate through these chapters, may you find insights, strategies, and inspiration to embark on a successful journey in the dynamic world of the Indian share market.

Happy reading, and may your investments soar with the Bulls and weather the storms with the Bears!